STUDY BIBLE

FOR

WOMEN

52-WEEK THEME
BASED SCRIPTURE READINGS
GUIDED BIBLE JOURNAL

ADISAN Publishing AB

EILEEN NYBERG

Table of Contents

Introduction

The New Living Translation (NLT) of the Bible was introduced in 1996. It is a translation of the Hebrew Bible and is an easy-to-understand version. Many other translations of the Bible had big, confusing words that people had trouble comprehending. The NLT version translated the other versions of the Bible into modern English, such as The Living Bible (TLB), published in 1971. The New Living Translation of the Bible is a new version of The Living Bible.

There is also a second edition of the NLT Bible that was published in 2007. The goal of the second edition was to help readers understand the text of the Bible even better. The writers of the NLT Bible wanted to make each passage as easy to read as possible. The result was a translation that was true to the original version of the Bible and acceptable to readers.

Currently, many people choose to read the New Living Translation of the Bible because it is one of the easiest versions to understand for personal and group Bible study. This translation allows each person to think deeply about each passage and how they relate to their lives. It also allows them to better understand what is being said in each passage to truly live the words of the Bible. The verses in the NLT Bible are different from other versions of the Bible.

Anyone can benefit from reading the NLT Bible. Adults will learn more about God using the NLT Bible as a guide in their everyday life. Adults can also read the NLT Bible to their children, so they can have a better understanding of God's word.

How to Read This Book

Being a woman is tough. You have many responsibilities. Those responsibilities range from work, taking care of your family, and taking care of yourself every day. It can become overwhelming. The good news is that God wants to take you into His arms and remind you that through Him, you are more than a conqueror. He wants you to have the faith, hope, determination, and perseverance to make it through any challenges that come your way.

This weekly NLT Study Bible aims to help you know God personally and apply His lessons in their daily lives. Each lesson has a Bible passage and explanation that every woman can relate to and put into practice in her life. There are discussion questions at the end of each lesson, which you can choose to journal about. Each question is designed to help you think about what you have learned through the week's lesson and how it can be applied in your life to develop a closer relationship with God.

The best way to go through this book is individually. Sit down with your Bible (this study is based on the New Living Translation or NLT), have a pen or pencil ready, maybe a cup of coffee, and commit a few moments of your day to walk through this study.

This year-long study Bible aims to help you realize there is nothing that you can't get through with God on your side.

We hope that women will be encouraged, strengthened, and uplifted in their faith walk with each weekly lesson.

Week 1

BLESSINGS FOR EVERYONE

SCRIPTURE READINGS:

Day One: Jeremiah 17:7-8 (Blessings for trusting in God)

Day Two: Proverbs 16:3 (Commit your plans to God)

Day Three: Ephesians 3:1-4 (God's mysterious plan)

Day Four: Deuteronomy 28:2 (Blessings will come upon you)

Day Five: Deuteronomy 28:13 (The head, not the tail)

Day Six: Proverbs 16:20 (Discover Good)

Day Seven: 2 Peter 1:3 (Divine power)

The Lord had said to Abram, "Leave your native country, your relatives, and your father's family, and go to the land that I will show you. [2] I will make you into a great nation. I will bless you and make you famous, and you will be a blessing to others. [3] I will bless those who bless you and curse those who treat you with contempt. All the families on earth will be blessed through you." Genesis 12:1-3

When the Lord tells you to go somewhere or to do something, do you question Him, or do you do exactly what He is telling you to do, right away, without any hesitation? As a woman, you are often told to do things in your life at a moment's notice by your husband, friends, co-workers, and even by your boss. Do you automatically do the things they tell you to do or figure out the best way to achieve the tasks they ask you to do first, so you don't run into problems later on? Often you may want to wait to see how things will play out for you instead of doing things right away. If acting right away means you will be changing offices or locations, you have to discuss those things with your family and figure out what is best for them. You also have to pack up everything you own and move with your family to a new location. That takes a lot of time, discipline, and patience to sell your house and find a new place to live. It also means saying goodbye to your friends and family members, and that can be hard on you too.

However, if God is putting it in your heart to do something or to move somewhere new, just as He told Abram to move to a new land, you also have to trust that God only wants what is best for you and your family. Even if you're afraid of the future, or afraid of what the new change in your life could bring, or what this new location for work will be, you can draw both courage and strength from this Bible passage. God told Abram that if he listened to Him, God would make him a great nation and that He would bless Abram. Maybe God is telling you to move to a new location or to go to a new job because He knows it will be a bigger blessing than what you may be receiving right now.

Take the time to pray and listen to God and realize what He has put on your heart. Just as He told Abram, He is putting you in your new position to be a blessing not only in your own life but also for you to be a blessing to many other people you will cross paths with in your faith walk. If God promised He would bless Abram and make him famous among the nations, imagine how much He can and will do for you if you walk in obedience to Him. You're allowed to pray and ask Him about where He wants you to go in life. Ask Him for guidance no matter where He is leading you. You can even ask yourself if you are letting God have control over your life, or are you trying to go through life at your own pace instead of God's? If you find yourself wondering and searching for answers, take the time to ask God what He wants you to do in your life. His answers will give you clarification, reassurance, and peace.

PRACTICAL APPLICATION:

Where has God been telling you to go in your life?

_____
_____
_____
_____

Have you willingly obeyed God and gone where He is telling you to go in your life?

_____
_____
_____
_____

How can you learn to let go of the reigns of your life and let God take the lead in your life?

_____
_____
_____
_____

In what ways can you let God lead you in your job, your family life, or your individual life?

_____
_____
_____
_____

ENGAGE YOUR MIND:

In what ways has God helped you trust that His plans are always better than yours?

_____
_____
_____
_____

What questions do you need to ask God about where He is leading you in your life?

_____

_____

_____

_____

What answers have you received from Him about taking a new job or moving somewhere new?

_____

_____

_____

_____

ENGAGE YOUR HEART:

How has God helped calm your anxieties about the new places He is telling you to go?

_____

_____

_____

_____

Week 2

WHAT DID GOD INTEND?

SCRIPTURE READINGS:

Day One: Psalm 119:1-3 (Blessed are the blameless)

Day Two: Psalm 126:5-6 (Reap with shouts of joy)

Day Three: Deuteronomy 28:3-6 (Blessings all around)

Day Four: Psalm 44:21 (God knows all)

Day Five: 2 Corinthians 9:8 (Provide all you need)

Day Six: Philippians 4:19 (Supply all your riches)

Day Seven: Numbers 6:24 (Blessings from God)

"You intended to harm me, but God intended it all for good. He brought me to this position so I could save the lives of many people." Genesis 50:20

From work to family issues, the list of things to worry about and think about seems never-ending. Even Joseph, as one of the rulers over Egypt, had things that worried him. He might have been worried about how he would feel when and if he faced his brothers again for the first time in many years. This is what our text for this Bible lesson is about. Joseph had seen his brothers when they journeyed to Egypt from Canaan to get food during the famine they were experiencing. Joseph finally admitted that he was their long-lost brother and that he wouldn't harm any of them. He even told them, "You might have intended to harm me, but God intended it for good…" Joseph recognized that God had him in that particular position for the good of many people. He was put in that position to save many people's lives, including the lives of the people he thought he hated -- his brothers. He thought he hated them and would hate them for the rest of his life, but God knew that he would see them again and end up saving them from starvation and certain death.

God knew He had a terrific and amazing plan for Joseph's life. He also has an amazing plan for your life too. Think about where God has placed you in your life. Where you are in your job right now is right where God wants you to be. You may not understand why you are in that position right now, but if you seek God in everything you do and ask Him for guidance and wisdom in every area of your life, you will get the answers you have been searching for. In time you will understand why things have happened in the way they did, and you will also understand how God has played a big impact in your life. He has put you in your current position to impact His kingdom, to be a witness for Him, and bring others to Him.

He has brought you through the hardest time of your life so that you can help inspire others to never give up no matter how hard things may seem for them. You were put in your family's life to teach them how to follow God and how to be a witness unto the next generation. In your job, you are called to be kind to those who are unkind to you, just as Joseph showed true kindness to his unkind brothers. You are to engage with others with the kindness that God has shown you in every area of your life.

You are on this earth to help others in the same ways that God has helped you. Remember, when others may have intended to harm you in some way, God is using those experiences as stepping stones that will help mold you into the person you are meant to be in life. When you see the light on the other side, God will reveal how He helped you through that tough time and how He shaped you into the person you are made to be in His eyes.

PRACTICAL APPLICATION:

What position of power has God placed you in, whether in your work life, personal, or family life? How can you make an impact for God's kingdom?

_____
_____
_____
_____
_____
_____

What can you do to impact other people's lives for the good of Christ? How can you help people see that God is working for good in their lives?

_____
_____
_____
_____
_____

How has God helped you show mercy and kindness in all of your interactions? What lessons did you learn from the story of Joseph?

_____
_____
_____
_____
_____

In what ways can you be like Joseph and forgive people who have hurt or harmed you?

_____
_____
_____
_____
_____

ENGAGE YOUR MIND:

How has He revealed to you that the things you thought would harm you in life were intended for your good?

_____

_____

_____

_____

_____

_____

ENGAGE YOUR HEART:

How do you feel when you show mercy to others?

_____

_____

_____

_____

_____

_____

Week 3

KEEP SUNDAY HOLY

SCRIPTURE READINGS:

Day One: Ezekiel 20:19-20 (A sign between you And God)

Day Two: Deuteronomy 5:12-14 (No work on Sundays)

Day Three: Genesis 2:3 (Sundays are holy)

Day Four: Isaiah 58:13-14 (Keep Sundays honorable)

Day Five: Mathew 12:12 (Do good on Sundays)

Day Six: Romans 14:5 (Each day is different)

Day Seven: Leviticus 23:3 (Rest on Sunday)

"8 Remember to observe the Sabbath day by keeping it holy." Exodus 20:8

This scripture is one of the hardest commandments to keep, not just for men but for women too. Life is in a constant movement, no matter where you may look and where you turn. Every day there is work to be done, bills to pay, cars to run and fix, groceries to buy, dinners and lunches to make for your family, and laundry to be sorted, cleaned, folded, and put away. Those things are just some of the busy work that comes with everyday life.

Since life is in a constant state of movement, you might wonder, "How do I take the time off on Sundays? How do I refocus my energy to relax enough on Sundays when I am so busy throughout the week?" You might even ask yourself, "Why is it so important that I take time off on Sundays? What benefit can it bring me if I rest on Sunday? Why is it a command that I rest on Sunday? I have so much work to do that I can't afford to take time off on Sundays."

The list of excuses as to why you can't take the time away from your work, chores, or housework could go on and on if you chose to let it. Satan makes you think that you can't take time off because if you do, you won't want to get the tasks done the next day. Satan can make you think that taking time off from work will not benefit you in the long run. That's a lie that he puts in your head.

On the contrary, you need to take a day off at least once a week to replenish yourself and give yourself some time to not think about anything. You need to allow yourself the time to rest and to relax. God even rested on the seventh day after He created the earth. If God can rest after creating the earth and everything in it, you too can rest on Sundays, no matter what you may have going on. You need time to let your mind and your body rest. It's important for your physical, mental, emotional, and spiritual health.

God wants you to remember the Sabbath day by keeping it holy, which means not doing any work on Sunday. As hard as it can seem to not do any work on Sunday, you can train yourself not to work on Sundays. Just do as much as you can on all the other days so you can rest on Sundays, but at the same time, don't work yourself to the bone. God doesn't want you to run yourself ragged, working on many different things at once. Rather He wants you to take things one step at a time, one hour at a time, even one second at a time. He also wants you to give yourself time to rest and recharge. You do not have to ever feel guilty about keeping the Sabbath holy by not doing anything on Sundays. God didn't feel guilty for not working on Sunday, so you don't need to feel guilty about it either. Give yourself time off every week so that way you're able to recharge for the new week that is ahead for you. That way, you can tackle every task with a clear head and with God at your side.

PRACTICAL APPLICATION:

How have you disobeyed God by working on the Sabbath? Did you even realize that you were disobeying God by working on the Sabbath?

_____

_____

_____

_____

_____

_____

_____

Have you ever felt like you couldn't take time away from work or other obligations on Sundays?

_____

_____

_____

_____

_____

_____

_____

ENGAGE YOUR MIND:

How can you change your attitude about not working on Sundays?

_____

_____

_____

_____

_____

_____

_____

How has your life changed for the better since you stopped working on Sundays?

_____
_____
_____
_____
_____
_____

ENGAGE YOUR HEART:

How do you feel knowing that you have disobeyed God by working on Sundays?

_____
_____
_____
_____
_____

How have you honored God by choosing not to work on Sundays?

_____
_____
_____
_____
_____

Week 4

PARDON FROM SIN

SCRIPTURE READINGS:

Day One: Mark 11:25 (Forgive others)

Day Two: 1 John 1:9 (Cleansed from unrighteousness)

Day Three: Acts 2:38 (Receive gifts from the Holy Spirit)

Day Four: Ephesians 4:32 (Be tenderhearted)

Day Five: Luke 6:37 (Forgive and you'll be forgiven)

Day Six: Mathew 21:18-22 (Seventy-seven times seven)

Day Seven: Acts 3:19 (Repent)

¹⁸ 'The Lord is slow to anger and filled with unfailing love, forgiving every kind of sin and rebellion. But he does not excuse the guilty. He lays the sins of the parents upon their children; the entire family is affected—even children in the third and fourth generations.' ¹⁹ In keeping with your magnificent, unfailing love, please pardon the sins of this people, just as you have forgiven them ever since they left Egypt."
Numbers 14:18-19

The Lord loves you and wants to forgive you of every sin that you commit. He forgives you of every sin and rebellion against Him. He will forgive you as long as you ask for forgiveness with all of your heart and mean that you are truly sorry for the sins that you've committed. However, He does not excuse those people who are guilty. This means that He doesn't excuse the people that haven't asked for forgiveness in their lives. The sins of every parent are upon their children. The entire family will be affected by sins, even the kids born in the third and fourth generations. He doesn't say those things to scare you. Rather He tells you these things to make you a wiser and a stronger individual.

He wants to help teach you and warn you of what happens when you sin every day. Every action has an equal and opposite reaction. Your kids may be affected by the things you do and say in your home life, your marriage, and the example that you show them every day. If they see you reacting to situations with anger, they too will react to certain situations with anger. However, if they see you react with calmness, clarity, and peace of mind in every situation, they too will react that same way in their everyday activities.

What you teach your kids and how you teach your kids matters. You can do your best not to show anger or other raw emotions in front of your kids that may affect them for the rest of their lives. When they see you react with anger, sorrow, or frustration, you can then use those times as teaching moments for your kids. You can teach them not to react in the same ways that you reacted. You can teach them to react with kindness in every situation, the same way that God reacts towards you in everything you do.

Later in these verses, Moses pleaded with God to spare the Israelites from their sins just as God had forgiven them ever since they left Egypt. The Lord is slow to anger, and He is also filled with unfailing love. Moses is pleading with God to keep His magnificent love for the Israelites and for Him to forgive the Israelites sins. Think back to when you pleaded with God to forgive you from your sins and be merciful to you. You sin every day, and there is very little you can do to avoid sinning. You will fail every day, no matter how hard you try not to sin. Things will be said out of anger, sadness, pure confusion, and you will be left wondering why you did and said certain things the way you did. You will sometimes be left reeling from the way you did things without God's help and how everything came crashing down around you because of your own selfish choices to sin. You can teach yourself to ask for forgiveness and mean it with all your heart. God will not fail to forgive you.

PRACTICAL APPLICATION:

What have you learned about sin? What did you learn about how sin affects everyone in your family from generation to generation?

_____

_____

_____

_____

In what ways can you and your family turn away from sin?

_____

_____

_____

_____

How has God shown His unfailing love and mercy to you even amid your darkest sin?

_____

_____

_____

_____

Have you ever pleaded with God to forgive your sins?

_____

_____

_____

_____

ENGAGE YOUR MIND:

In what ways have you tried to hide your sins from God or other people? Has someone ever interceded on your behalf, just like Moses interceded for the Israelites?

_____

_____

_____

_____

In what ways have you asked for forgiveness from your sins every day?

_____

_____

_____

_____

_____

_____

ENGAGE YOUR HEART:

Have you ever felt so guilty that you couldn't approach God without tears in your eyes and sorrow in your heart?

_____

_____

_____

_____

_____

How did it feel being freed from the guilt and shame of your sins by God?

_____

_____

_____

_____

_____

Week 5

BLESSINGS OF OBEDIENCE

SCRIPTURE READINGS:

Day One: Romans 2:13 (Doers of the Word)

Day Two: Deuteronomy 30:2 (Return to the Lord)

Day Three: Isaiah 1:9 (Consent and obey)

Day Four: 1 Samuel 15:22 (Obeying Is better than sacrifices)

Day Five: John 9:31 (God fearers)

Day Six: Deuteronomy 6:25 (Obtain righteousness)

Day Seven: Acts 5:32 (Witnesses)

I f you've ever been nervous about obeying God and about doing what He was telling you to do, you aren't the only one who has felt that way. Every woman on earth has had moments of doubt in her life, whether it was doubts about her career, her marriage, her kids, her kids' education, her family's health, and just about everything else in between. Have you ever wondered what would happen if you obeyed God fully and took that leap of faith for your family, in your career, or that leap of faith to help your kids in school? When you obey Him, He smiles on you. Good things will happen to those who obey Him. You will be blessed in more ways than you can fathom when you choose to follow God where He is leading you in your life. Let that realization cover you like a warm blanket. If you do what He asks of you willingly, your life will be blessed.

He didn't say, "Your life can be blessed if you obey me," or "Your life might be blessed if you obey me," or "I'll think about blessing you if you obey me." No. He said, "I will bless you if you obey my commandments." God also said, "If you obey my commandments, I will bless you and set you high above the nations of this world." In today's day and age, it could mean that He will bless you with the ability to lead others to Christ in your family life or your work life. It could also mean that He will give you the ability to be a natural Christ-like leader in any position that He puts you in at your job. It could also mean that your friends will be inspired to devote their lives to Christ through you. If you willingly obey God, He will not only bless you. He will bless your family, your friends, your extended family, and your job.

Whatever you do will be blessed as long as you keep your eyes on God and keep the faith, no matter how hard things will get. God has an awesome plan for your life, and He will help you achieve your goals and dreams as long as you do your best to stay close to Him every day. There is nothing like giving up on your plans for your life and willingly going where God wants you to go in your life. There is the ultimate peace that surpasses all human understanding when you obey Him. You will feel peace in your heart that only comes from knowing Him. Knowing that He will guide you and bless your life will help you make even better decisions about your marriage, career, and where your kids go to school. Your family life, work, marriage, extended family, and even your individual life will be blessed when you obey God's commands to the best of your ability. You will be blessed in more ways than you can fathom, think of, or imagine.

PRACTICAL APPLICATION:

What commands has God given you to follow?

_____
_____
_____
_____
_____
_____

How did you overcome the hesitation to follow Him? What made you hesitant in following Him? How did God bless you when you followed Him?

_____
_____
_____
_____
_____
_____

Has your marriage, family, extended family, or work environment been blessed by your willingness to go where God has led you?

_____
_____
_____
_____
_____
_____

Did this passage bring you comfort, knowing that if you obey God, He will bless you in more ways than you could ever think possible?

_____
_____
_____
_____
_____
_____

ENGAGE YOUR MIND:

Where have you willingly obeyed God in your faith walk? Where in your faith walk is it hard to obey God sometimes?

_____

_____

_____

_____

_____

_____

_____

_____

ENGAGE YOUR HEART:

Have you willingly surrendered your life to God's plan instead of thinking your plan was better? How did it feel willingly surrendering to God's plan?

_____

_____

_____

_____

_____

_____

_____

_____

Week 6

MAKING VOWS

SCRIPTURE READINGS:

Day One: Deuteronomy 23: 21-23(Fulfil vows)

Day Two: James 5:12 (Let Your Yes be yes)

Day Three: Ecclesiastes 5:4-6 (Pay for your vows)

Day Four: Numbers 30:12 (Don't break vows)

Day Five: Psalm 61:8 (Sing praises)

Day Six: Psalm 76:11 (Bring gifts to God)

Day Seven: Job 22:27 (Pray and God hears your vows)

"If a young woman makes a vow to the Lord or a pledge under oath while she is still living at her father's home, ⁴ and her father hears of the vow or pledge and does not object to it, then all her vows and pledges will stand." Numbers 30:3-4

If a woman makes a vow to the Lord or swears under oath while she is still living in her father's house, and her father hears the vow and doesn't say anything against it, any vow the woman makes will stand before her heavenly Father and her earthly father. If you ever make a vow to do something in front of your father, see whether or not he objects to it because if he objects to it, then it won't stand. If he doesn't object to it, then it will stay in place. Be careful whenever you speak out loud in front of your father because he has the power to have the final word over anything you say.

This lesson teaches women everywhere to watch the things they say in front of their earthly father and even more so to watch the things they say in front of God, as He is their heavenly Father. Think back to a time when you said in front of your father or anyone in your life, "I swear that…." God not only hears you say that, but He also doesn't want you to swear to anything. Rather, He wants you to tell the truth in everything you say.

Remember, making a vow is different from swearing to God. When you make a vow, God wants you to honor it. When you commit to someone to, let's say, go over to their house for dinner, or help them clean their house, do not back out of that agreement or have second thoughts about it. Rather than backing out of that agreement, God wants you to honor the commitment you made to that person.

When you say, "I swear on," or "I swear to God that…" you are swearing by God's authority that you're going to do something or that something happened. You're trying to use God's authority in your earthly body and mind. Remember, it is never good to say, "I swear to God…" because you don't have the authority to be God. Only God is God. Only God has the authority and power to say things did or didn't happen. Remember, God sees all and knows all, so you always have to be careful not to say you swear to God about something.

God has given your earthly father eyes to see and ears to hear everything that you say, even as you journey from his house and venture out on your own as an adult. When you were younger, your father would scold you for saying things that were out of turn or saying things in a disrespectful manner to him or anyone else. God put your earthly father in that very place of authority so he could teach you throughout your life to not swear on God or swear to God about anything in front of your friends. Let your father teach you that it's not good to swear to God about anything. Let your father also teach you that it's better to honor your vows and commitments than cancel them or not go through with them.

PRACTICAL APPLICATION:

Have you ever made a vow or said "I swear that..." or "I swear to God that..." in front of your dad?

_____
_____
_____
_____
_____
_____

How did your dad react to hearing you say that as a young kid? Did he ever teach you not to say, "I swear that..."?

_____
_____
_____
_____
_____
_____

When you were younger, did your dad ever teach you how you should always honor every commitment you make with people?

_____
_____
_____
_____
_____
_____

What is the most important piece of advice your father has given you?

_____
_____
_____
_____
_____
_____

What other things has God helped you learn through your earthly father's wisdom and knowledge?

_____

_____

_____

_____

_____

_____

ENGAGE YOUR MIND:

What have you learned through this lesson about making vows in front of God and your earthly father?

_____

_____

_____

_____

_____

ENGAGE YOUR HEART:

How does it feel knowing that you should always keep commitments to people? How does it feel to be keeping the vows in your marriage?

_____

_____

_____

_____

_____

Week 7

WHO WILL YOU SERVE?

SCRIPTURE READINGS:

Day One: 1 Samuel 12:24 (Serve God faithfully)

Day Two: Colossians 3:23-24 (Work heartedly for God)

Day Three: 1 Corinthians 15:58 (Abound in work for God)

Day Four: Mathew 6:24 (You can't serve two masters)

Day Five: Romans 12:2 (Spiritual worship)

Day Six: Mark 10:45 (He came to serve)

Day Seven: Deuteronomy 13:4 (Serve God)

"But if you refuse to serve the Lord, then choose today whom you will serve. Would you prefer the gods your ancestors served beyond the Euphrates? Or will it be the gods of the Amorites in whose land you now live? But as for me and my family, we will serve the Lord." Joshua 24:15

Have you ever seen anyone you know and love refuse to know Jesus or serve Him? You have to make a conscious choice of whom you will serve every day of your life. Remember, you can't serve two masters. You can only serve one master, and it should be God. Many women everywhere have to make that choice as to whom they will serve every day. They may choose to serve their husbands, their kids, even their bosses. If they choose to serve someone other than God, they will run into more trouble.

This Bible verse even goes into detail about what other gods people may have chosen to serve. They were given a choice from Joshua, Moses' appointed successor, whom they could serve. They were given a choice to serve the gods their ancestors served beyond the Euphrates or to serve the gods of the Amorites in the land they lived in at that time. You also have that choice to make every day of your life. You have to figure out whom you will serve. Either you will serve God, or you won't serve Him. You can't be lukewarm about serving God and then suddenly change your mind about it. You have to make the conscious effort to serve the Lord every day for the good of yourself, your family, your friends, and even your coworkers and your boss. You can impact them every day of your life just by walking with God in everything you say and do.

Make the conscious effort to serve God in everything you do, especially in your words and actions with other people. Be willing to go the extra mile for those around you, even when they can't pay you back for your kindness. Wake up every day saying, "I choose you, Lord. You are the Lord over my life. I give everything that I'm going to do up to You. Help me to serve You willingly and to serve others even when I will get nothing in return. When I fail and fall away from You, Lord, please forgive me for my shortcomings. Please lead me back to You and help me to stay steadfast in You and Your love. Please help me to teach my children that knowing You is the best decision they will ever make in their lives. Please help me lead by example through Your power and might. Help me to be Your example in everything I do and say. Help me to want to willingly serve You, just as Your servant Joshua did."

When you make an effort to serve God every day, your life will be blessed more than you could fathom. Have you ever noticed that when your mind goes off track that things get more difficult for you? Satan makes it that much more difficult to return to God because you feel as though you may not be able to serve Him. Don't believe what Satan puts in your head. You can return to serving God with all your heart and make a difference in your life and the lives of those around you. If someone ever asks you whom you serve, you can be bold like Joshua and say, "As for me and my house, we will serve the Lord."

PRACTICAL APPLICATION:

Whom do you serve daily?

_____
_____
_____
_____
_____
_____
_____
_____

Has anyone ever asked you why you serve God? What was your reaction to that person's question? How did you explain to them why it's so important to serve God?

_____
_____
_____
_____
_____
_____
_____
_____

What was your reaction to realizing that you fall short of God's mark every single day, even when you do your best to serve Him?

_____
_____
_____
_____
_____
_____
_____
_____

ENGAGE YOUR MIND:

Do you serve God willingly every day, or do you have to remind yourself to serve Him? How can you change your mindset to serve Him willingly?

_____
_____
_____
_____
_____
_____
_____
_____

ENGAGE YOUR HEART:

How does it feel to serve God every day?

_____
_____
_____
_____
_____
_____
_____
_____

Week 8

REJOICE IN THE LORD

SCRIPTURE READINGS:

Day One: Philippians 4:14 (Rejoice in the Lord)

Day Two: Psalm 113:1-9 (Praise the Lord)

Day Three: Luke 10:20 (Rejoice, your name is written in Heaven)

Day Four: Isaiah 61:10 (Exult your God)

Day Five: Romans 12:15 (Rejoice with those who rejoice)

Day Six: Luke 15:10 (Angels rejoice over repentance)

Day Seven: Zephaniah 3:14-17 (Rejoice with all your heart)

"My heart rejoices in the Lord! The Lord has made me strong. Now I have an answer for my enemies; I rejoice because you rescued me. ²No one is holy like the Lord! There is no one besides you; there is no Rock like our God." 1 Samuel 2:1-2

You can rejoice in the goodness of God no matter what may be going on in your life. Even if your life is full of storm clouds and you're left wondering what to do in certain situations, you can still find the beauty amongst the chaos and choose to worship God through these difficult circumstances. Even when it's hard to keep faith in your life, you can remind yourself of the many other times God has gotten you through storms. You can be thankful for the many valuable lessons each storm in your life has taught you. Think back; what is the darkest time you ever faced in your life? How did you hold on to God during that dark time? How did you see the glimmer of hope even through the darkness? God is still with you, even in your darkest moments. Even though it can be very hard to see, feel, and trust Him in those types of moments, remember that He *is* always with you and that He *was* always with you. No matter what you faced before, He got you through, and He will get you through the darkness again. He is your lighthouse in the storm. He is the hope that you can cling to no matter how hopeless things may seem.

You can say things like, "My heart rejoices in the Lord! The Lord is making me strong, and He has already made me strong," or "No matter what comes my way, I know God will get me through," or "No matter who may attack me as my enemy, I have an answer for my enemies."

You may also say, "I rejoice because I know God has gotten me through another difficult time," and "I'm grateful for all the lessons I've learned through the struggles that I have faced so far in my life. I'm grateful that I have You to learn from and lean on, Lord!"

You can help your friends or family members, who may be going through a hard time, to learn how they can trust in God. You can boldly say, "No one is holy like the Lord. There is no one besides You, Lord; there is no Rock like our God." When you say those words of affirmation, you are giving people an open invitation to believe in the goodness of God. You are proclaiming the good things that He has done for you in your life. You are proclaiming His love for you and your love for Him.

When you boldly declare how good He is, people may stop and stare at you. Don't worry about what they think or what they might say to you. Rather keep declaring the goodness of God over your life, no matter what, and no matter who looks at you in a weird way. If you keep declaring how good God is even in the darkest of times, you will get through those times with a lot more clarity and peace than if you lamented in the way things were going in your life. There is nothing wrong with shouting it from the rooftops about how good God has been to you. If you keep declaring how good God is, you will see His hand in everything, and you will be able to rejoice in Him no matter the difficulties you face in your life.

PRACTICAL APPLICATION:

What difficulties have you faced in your life that made it hard for you to trust in God?

_____

_____

_____

_____

_____

_____

In what ways have you shown your appreciation for His work in your life?

_____

_____

_____

_____

_____

_____

Are you bold enough to tell the world that God is the only reason why you have made it this far?

_____

_____

_____

_____

_____

_____

How did God help you realize that He is for you, not against you?

_____

_____

_____

_____

_____

_____

ENGAGE YOUR MIND:

In what areas of your life do you need to trust God more?

_____

_____

_____

_____

_____

_____

Are you ready to willingly surrender all trust to God?

_____

_____

_____

_____

_____

_____

ENGAGE YOUR HEART:

How does it feel knowing that you can rejoice in God even in the middle of your struggles?

_____

_____

_____

_____

_____

Week 9

DELIVERANCE FROM YOUR ENEMIES

SCRIPTURE READINGS:

Day One: Luke 1:71 (Saved from your enemies)

Day Two: Psalm 18:17 (Rescue from enemies)

Day Three: Acts 16:31 (You'll be saved)

Day Four: 2 Samuel 22:18 (Rescue)

Day Five: Galatians 5:1 (Christ has set you free)

Day Six: Ephesians 2:8 (Gift of God)

Day Seven: Psalm 51:1 (Bought from iniquity)

"He reached down from heaven and rescued me; he drew me out of deep waters.18 He rescued me from my powerful enemies, from those who hated me and were too strong for me." 2 Samuel 22: 17-18

What has God rescued you from? Think back to a time when you thought there was no way you could hold on for another day. God brought you through that moment. He has done so much to rescue you. He has offered you His never-ending grace, mercy, love, forgiveness, and most importantly, He has offered you eternal salvation through faith in Jesus Christ. If you have accepted Jesus as your Savior, you know that you have an eternal place in Heaven waiting for you. No matter what happens in your life, and no matter how hard things get, you have a glorious eternity waiting for you. Let that thought excite you and even tingle your senses. Let that thought sink into your mind. You have a place in Heaven waiting for you with Jesus. When you get to Heaven, there will be no more sorrow, pain, or anxiety. There will be no more turmoil. There will only be joy and praising God for eternity.

Think about the deep waters He has rescued you from. They could be the pits of depression or suicidal thoughts. They also could have been moments of anger at yourself or frustration for not doing everything correctly the first time. You might be lonely and longing for friendships. God's not deaf or blind to any of your thoughts. He knows the thoughts that are in your head even before you think any of them. He even knows when certain thoughts will come into your mind. He can and will heal you from any destructive thoughts that come into your mind. All you have to do is ask Him to change your thought process towards Him. Ask Him to reveal what He thinks of you and to save you from sabotaging negative self-talk.

He has delivered you from the hands of your enemies. He has kept you from so many different things that could have done you harm. Remember the times you were late to a meeting at work? God had you be late for a reason, and He could have been protecting you from an earlier wreck that happened on the road. Remember when your son or daughter called you saying that they weren't feeling well in school? You rushed to pick them up and find out what was wrong, and your boss gave you the time to get them home safely and take care of them. Remember when you weren't sure how you would pay your mortgage and how God gave you an unexpected blessing to help you pay your bills? God has brought you through many of those types of trials, and He has even helped you avoid many trials in your life.

Do you remember the time someone at work said something mean or that was harmful to your reputation? God may have told you not to speak out against them, so you didn't damage your reputation any further. God helped you stay silent so you didn't lose your job by inappropriately speaking out at the wrong time.

God has also helped you know when to speak out against your enemies. He has helped give you the right words at the right time and in the right place. He has helped you know when it's appropriate to open your mouth and when it's appropriate to remain silent. He can and will deliver you from the enemies that seem to be too strong for you.

PRACTICAL APPLICATION:

What has God saved you from in your life? How has He helped you stop negative self-sabotage?

_____
_____
_____
_____
_____
_____
_____

Have you ever thought that your enemies were too strong for you?

_____
_____
_____
_____
_____
_____
_____

ENGAGE YOUR MIND:

In what ways have you tried to save yourself from your enemies instead of relying on God and asking Him for help?

_____
_____
_____
_____
_____
_____

How can you change your thinking and realize that you need to have a dependence on God?

_____

_____

_____

_____

_____

_____

_____

ENGAGE YOUR HEART:

How does it feel when you realize that you already have complete power over your enemies? How does it feel knowing you already have victory in Christ?

_____

_____

_____

_____

_____

_____

_____

_____

_____

Week 10

SUCH A TIME AS THIS

SCRIPTURE READINGS:

Day One: Proverbs 16:9 (God establishes your steps)

Day Two: Jeremiah 1:5 (God knew you)

Day Three: Ephesians 2:10 (God's workmanship)

Day Four: Romans 8:28 (Called according to His purpose)

Day Five: Job 42:2 (God's purpose can't be stopped)

Day Six: Philippians 1:6 (He began a good work in you)

Day Seven: Psalm 138:8 (Fulfil His Purpose)

Esther was a young girl who had become queen at an early age. King Xerces had sent word that every eligible woman was to come before him to see which of those women he would make his queen. He found much favor with Esther, and he declared her queen. Esther learned of a horrible plot that was ready to be carried out against her, her family, and the entire Jewish community. Haman, the king's right-hand man, wanted to destroy Mordecai, who was the man that saved King Xerces' life. Haman was jealous of Mordecai because the king had found favor with him. Haman wanted to kill Mordecai and his entire family, which included Esther and all Jews.

Mordecai learned that Haman wanted to kill all of them. He went to tell Esther that she needed to act quickly to save herself and her family. Esther, however, was afraid. She didn't want to go to the king and request an audience with him unannounced. She knew the punishment for showing up in front of the king unannounced was death, even though she was the queen. She had every right to be afraid of talking to the king.

She expressed her fears to Mordecai, and he told her not to think that just because she was in a position of power as the queen, she would escape when all the other Jews were killed. He also told her that if she kept quiet, the deliverance for the Jews would come from another place. He warned her still that even if the deliverance would come from another place, she and her family would still die. He then left her with the thought that she was put in the position of power as the queen just so she could save herself, her family, and the entire Jewish community from the demise of Haman.

After Esther had considered all of the possibilities and prayed, she knew she had to go before the king and tell him of Haman's plot against the Jews to save all of her people from death. She knew she couldn't just keep silent. She knew that it was in God's plan for her to save her family.

You can also summon up the same courage that Esther had. You can boldly come before God and ask Him what His divine purpose is for your life. You can ask Him for specifics on what He wants you to do. He wants you to boldly approach Him and ask Him for the courage that you need to do specific tasks. If you're afraid to talk about certain subjects with your husband, ask Him for the courage to bring certain topics up in a way that is pleasing to Him. If you're being treated unfairly at work, ask Him for the courage and the right time to speak to the right person about the things you're experiencing. If you see your kids struggling in school, ask God for ways in which you can help them. Assume the courage that Esther had and approach people, no matter how afraid you might be. God is going to be with you in every situation.

PRACTICAL APPLICATION:

In what areas have you been told to act, just as Esther was instructed to act?

_____

_____

_____

_____

_____

_____

How do you assume the courage to make the right people aware of difficult things in your life?

_____

_____

_____

_____

_____

_____

How did God answer your specific prayer requests and lead you to make the right decisions in your life?

_____

_____

_____

_____

_____

_____

ENGAGE YOUR MIND:

Are you in a position of power in your life right now?

_____

_____

_____

_____

_____

_____

In what ways has God revealed to you that He put you in this particular position to help lead others to Him?

_____
_____
_____
_____
_____
_____

How can you boldly assume the courage that Esther had even during certain death?

_____
_____
_____
_____
_____
_____

ENGAGE YOUR HEART:

How do you feel knowing that you can play a part in helping someone know Christ? How do you feel knowing that you can save someone's life?

_____
_____
_____
_____
_____
_____

Week 11

SHELTER OF THE MOST HIGH

SCRIPTURE READINGS:

Day One: Psalm 34:7-9 (Take refuge in God)

Day Two: 1 Thessalonians 3:3-5 (Strengthen and protection from God)

Day Three: Isaiah 54:17 (No weapon will prevail)

Day Four: Psalm 17:7-8 (Apple of God's eye)

Day Five: Isaiah 41:10 (Righteous right hand)

Day Six: Deuteronomy 31:6 (God will never leave you or forsake you)

Day Seven: 2 Timothy 4:18-20 (The Lord will rescue you)

"Those who live in the shelter of the Most-High will find rest in the shadow of the Almighty." Psalm 91:1

Have you ever wondered what it would be like to live in perfect peace all the days of your life? That is what God offers you in His presence. He invites you to come to Him no matter what you are dealing with, no matter how you feel. He wants you to come before Him crying out to Him. He already sees and knows all things. He knows that you will be fighting for your life and fighting for your faith at certain times. He knows what will happen in your life even before things happen. He knows when things will get you overwhelmed. He wants you to know that you can come to Him and tell Him what is on your mind and what thoughts are in your heart. He doesn't ever find fault with you for crying out to Him in the middle of tough situations. He would rather you come to Him than to ever turn away from Him. He doesn't want to see you suffering. He wants to help you through your difficult times.

He wants you to find rest in His promises and His word. He wants you to rest assured that He is always with you no matter what may be happening. He even says those people who dwell or live in the Most High shelter will dwell among Him and dwell under His protection. Who wouldn't want to live under God's holy protection every day of their life? Finding rest in God's arms is exactly what you may need in your life. Take the time and re-examine your heart and your life. Where have you been stressing out? Where do you need rest and reassurance? Maybe you need rest from your everyday work routine, patience among your family, or in your marriage. Maybe you need more love between you and your husband or children. Ask God where you need to find rest in Him in every area of your life, and He will reveal those things to you. It may not be right away, but He will reveal those things to you in His time. Be careful what you ask for, though. He may reveal things you didn't expect to find out about yourself.

Think about the stressors in your life. Ask yourself what you can do to eliminate some of those daily or weekly stressors to help you feel calm. Ask God to help you dwell under His refuge when things start to become too much to handle. Even before things start to spiral out of control, come to God in prayer, asking Him for clarity, peace of mind, and a calm heart. If you start asking Him for help in different areas of your life, before everything starts spiraling out of control, you will be able to remind yourself to also dwell in His secret place even when things seem as if they are too hard to handle. You will be able to tackle each new day with focus, clarity, and perseverance that you may not have had before. If you rest in His presence every day, you will gain new wisdom and new insight. Enjoy learning more about Him and willingly rest in His presence. Resting in His presence means willingly surrendering everything in your life over to Him daily.

PRACTICAL APPLICATIONS:

Where do you need to rest in God's presence? Is it in your work life, your home life, your marriage, or even in your spirituality?

_____
_____
_____
_____
_____
_____

What makes it hard to dwell in the secret of the Most High?

_____
_____
_____
_____
_____
_____

ENGAGE YOUR MIND:

What does dwelling in the shadow of the Almighty mean to you?

_____
_____
_____
_____
_____
_____

How can you remind yourself to constantly turn to God and rest in His presence? How can you switch your mind to turn to God instead of thinking negatively?

_____
_____
_____
_____

ENGAGE YOUR HEART:

How do you feel when you have trouble trusting God?

_____

_____

_____

_____

_____

_____

How can you calm your restless heart?

_____

_____

_____

_____

_____

_____

How can you ask God to calm your spirit no matter what you may be facing?

_____

_____

_____

_____

_____

_____

Week 12

DWELL WITH THE MOST HIGH

SCRIPTURE READINGS:

Day One: Ephesians 6: 10-15 (Be strong in the Lord)

Day Two: Proverbs 18:10-12 (Fortified tower)

Day Three: Psalm 121:7-8 (Kept safe from all harm)

Day Four: Psalm 32:7 (Hiding place)

Day Five: Psalm 3:3-5 (Shield)

Day Six: Isaiah 43:2 (Deep waters)

Day Seven: Psalm 16:11 (Path of life)

² "This I declare about the Lord: He alone is my refuge, my place of safety; he is my God, and I trust him. ³ For he will rescue you from every trap and protect you from deadly disease." Psalm 91: 2-3

od will rescue you from every trap that Satan and any of your other enemies have set against you. Satan has traps for you at every turn of your life. They can be traps for you mentally, physically, emotionally, and even spiritually. Satan wants you to turn away from God and think that your life is over whenever things get tough. He wants you to think that there is nothing left to live for when things start going wrong. Satan has sick ways of getting into your mind and making you completely forget about all the promises that God has told you throughout your life. Satan can play tricks on your mind, spirituality, and even your body if you give him the green light to attack you. But you don't have to let Him attack you. You have the power of the Holy Spirit at work within you. Use it to your advantage.

Say God's promises out loud, "I am His child. No harm will come near me.", "God has gotten me through many other hard times. I know this time it will not be any different.", "God is in control over every situation." and "No matter how raw my emotions may feel at any time, I have to keep believing that God has an awesome plan for my life."

Think about the other promises God has told you, such as "You are my child.", "You are my daughter.", "I am always with you.", "I'm never far away.", "I will never leave you or forsake you.", "There is nothing to fear." and "You are not alone in your journey." Those reassurances can be found in His Word, and most likely, He has had your family or friends say those very words to you. He has helped them all be a beacon of light in the middle of your darkest times, and He has allowed His words to be spoken to you through all of those special people in your life. At times you probably didn't want to listen to the things they said, but God was still working in your life at that time, even when you thought He wasn't anywhere near you. When you thought He was absent or not paying attention to your cries, or even thought that He didn't care what was happening in your life, God was still with you.

There are statements in this lesson that you can declare boldly over your own life. God alone is your refuge. He is your place of safety at all times. He is your God, and you can trust Him. He will and can protect you from all harm, and He will protect you from any deadly diseases that stalk their prey on the earth. He will protect you from Satan and his evil plots for your life as long as you continually trust in Him.

Declare His promises over your life! Say things like the following:

"I can do more than I ever thought possible through Christ who gives me strength."

"God alone is my refuge."

"In Him alone, I will trust. I won't trust myself to get out of tough situations because I know that God can and will deliver me from my stress, and I never have to face anything alone."

"He is my refuge, and I'm kept safe, even if I don't feel safe."

"He is always surrounding me with His angels, and He is protecting me from physical, emotional, mental, and all spiritual harm."

PRACTICAL APPLICATIONS:

What are some of the promises of God that you have declared over your life? What is your favorite promise from God?

_____

_____

_____

_____

_____

_____

_____

ENGAGE YOUR MIND:

In what areas of your life do you need the reassurance of God's blessings in your life?

_____

_____

_____

_____

_____

_____

_____

_____

How can you help yourself trust in God at all times?

_____

_____

_____

_____

_____

_____

_____

ENGAGE YOUR HEART:

Do you truly believe that God is your place of safety? How do you feel realizing that God is your safe place?

_____
_____
_____
_____
_____
_____
_____
_____
_____
_____

How can you surrender to God's loving arms every day of your life?

_____
_____
_____
_____
_____
_____
_____
_____
_____
_____

Week 13

HOW TO GAIN WISDOM

SCRIPTURE READINGS:

Day One: James 1:5 (Ask God for wisdom)

Day Two: James 3:17 (Wisdom from above)

Day Three: Proverbs 3:13-18 (Better than silver or gold)

Day Four: Proverbs 1:7 (Fear of the Lord)

Day Five: Ephesians 5:15-17 (Will of God)

Day Six: Proverbs 19:20 (Listen to advice)

Day Seven: Proverbs 10:23 (Wisdom is pleasure)

There is nothing wrong with crying out to God for insight on where to go or asking Him what you should do in your life. You are allowed to call on Him any time, whether it's day or night, and ask Him for guidance in your life. He wants you to cry out to Him in everyday situations, not just when things are difficult. He wants to hear your cries and shouts of praise when things in your life are working out. He longs for you to tell Him how grateful you are for His many blessings in your life. He smiles on you regardless of your situation. He wants you to call on Him, no matter what is on your mind.

He is not burdened by you crying out to Him whenever your heart is shattered. Whenever things get too hard for you to take, He is always there for you. He holds you in the palm of His hands every day. Even when you don't understand why things are happening, rest assured that He knows why things are happening the way they are. Whenever things aren't going the way you would like them to go, turn to Him for reassurance, wisdom, and understanding. He will reveal everything you need to know in His timing and His very own specific way. When you aren't sure which path to take in your career or marriage, call out to Him. He will guide you. You can approach Him about anything and everything in your life.

You can do things to tune your heart into the things that God may be revealing to you. You can read His word or devotionals every day. You can also set aside a specific time of the day to just have quiet time with just you and Him. He wants you to come into His presence at any time. Whenever you have quiet time with Him, tell Him what you're struggling with, in your life. Ask Him to reveal what path you should take.

Don't be afraid to cry out to Him from the depths of your heart for understanding. Boldly come before Him and ask Him for wisdom no matter what you want to know. God even said He enjoys the bold prayers of His children, so boldly approach Him no matter what you go through. Ask Him for wisdom in every area of your life, in your children's education, your family dynamics, your work life, and in your marriage. Even ask Him for the wisdom in navigating a new job and getting along with your new boss and coworkers. Nothing is too big or too small to approach God about. He already knows and sees all, so you may as well ask Him for the things you want to know. If you have ever been afraid to approach God and ask Him for wisdom and understanding, make that your prayer request. Ask God to help you get rid of the fear of asking for specific things in your life. Remind yourself that God enjoys hearing specific prayer requests from His children. Nothing that you ask for could ever surprise Him.

PRACTICAL APPLICATIONS:

What can you do daily to gain wisdom from God? What areas of your life do you need wisdom and guidance?

_____
_____
_____
_____
_____
_____

Have you turned your wonderings into specific prayer requests for wisdom?

_____
_____
_____
_____
_____

ENGAGE YOUR MIND:

How do you clear your mind of the negative thoughts that Satan can put in your head?

_____
_____
_____
_____
_____
_____

How do you get your mind ready to receive the wisdom that God gives you?

_____
_____
_____
_____
_____

Do you have conversations with God daily?

_____
_____
_____
_____
_____
_____

ENGAGE YOUR HEART:

Have you developed a quiet time for just you and God? What time of day
do you talk to Him?

_____
_____
_____
_____
_____
_____

How does it feel spending one on one time with God every day? How has
it changed your life?

_____
_____
_____
_____
_____
_____

What amazing things has God revealed to you when you ask for wisdom?

_____
_____
_____
_____
_____

Week 14

WISDOM FROM GOD

SCRIPTURE READINGS:

Day One: Proverbs 18:15 (Ear of the wise)

Day Two: Proverbs 2:6 (Knowledge and understanding)

Day Three: Proverbs 17:27-28 (Keep your cool)

Day Four: Luke 21:15 (God gives wisdom)

Day Five: Proverbs 11:12 (Humble wisdom)

Day Six: Psalm 90:12 (Heart of wisdom)

Day Seven: James 3:13 (Meekness of wisdom)

"Then you will understand what it means to fear the Lord, and you will gain knowledge of God.⁶ For the Lord grants wisdom! From his mouth come knowledge and understanding." Proverbs 2:5-6

You might be wondering what it means to fear the Lord. To fear Him doesn't mean that you are afraid of Him. No. Rather it means that you know Him on a deeply personal level. Knowing God is the most important decision you will ever make in your life. Once you get to know Him, you will gain a lot of knowledge about Him. You will know His ways and how His ways are better than your ways. Your ways may seem right for you at any specific time, but once you pray for the Lord to work in your life, you will be able to understand Him on a much deeper level.

Some ways that you can easily gain wisdom are by engaging with other believers in a Bible study, praying for and with other believers, going to church, reading your Bible or reading daily devotionals every day, and finding quiet time with just you and the Lord, even if your day is extremely busy. You can also find the time to pray for specific needs of those around you or specific needs in your personal life. There is nothing wrong with being specific in your prayer requests. He wants you to ask for wisdom throughout your life because He wants you to learn more about Him every single day. He can and will reveal a thing to you that you never thought possible.

Think about the things that you want to know in your life. Maybe you want to try to make new friends but are too shy to have conversations with people. God can reveal new and exciting ways that you can make new Godly friends that will stay true to you. Maybe you know it's time to make a change in your life and step away from your family's abusive patterns, yet you're afraid and unsure of how to get out of that situation. God will reveal the best way out of that situation, and the best time you should get yourself out of that situation. Maybe you know it's time to get a new job, yet you aren't sure where to look or apply. God will reveal the right time to leave your current job. He will give you peace of mind about searching for a new one. He will help you know where to apply for a new job based on your skills and talents.

Maybe you want to try and reconnect with your spouse after some time of falling apart from each other. God will give you the wisdom to approach your husband with love, respect, and a calm manner. If it is His will, He will allow you both to rekindle the love and respect you had at one time for one another. Everything will happen as long as it is His will.

From the Lord's mouth comes wisdom, knowledge, and understanding. After all, He knows everything already, so there is no harm in asking for wisdom to be transferred from His mind to your mind. He can and will reveal many things to you in your lifetime, but He will do so in His own very specific ways. You also have to open your mind and be ready to receive the wisdom you're asking for.

PRACTICAL APPLICATIONS:

In what ways have you relied on your knowledge in your life?

_____
_____
_____
_____
_____
_____

Do you seek wisdom with your power, or do you seek wisdom through God's power?

_____
_____
_____
_____
_____
_____

Have you asked God for wisdom in your life? What has He revealed to you?

_____
_____
_____
_____
_____
_____

ENGAGE YOUR MIND:

In what ways has God revealed His wisdom to you through prayer and petition?

_____
_____
_____
_____
_____

What must you change in your thinking to receive wisdom from God?

_____
_____
_____
_____
_____

ENGAGE YOUR HEART:

Have you ever felt skeptical about asking Him for wisdom in a specific part of your life? What makes you skeptical about approaching God?

_____
_____
_____
_____
_____

How did it feel to open your heart to receive wisdom from God?

_____
_____
_____
_____
_____

Week 15

WHAT IS RIGHT?

SCRIPTURE READINGS:

Day One: James 4:17 (Not doing right)

Day Two: Roman's 12:21 (Overcome evil with good)

Day Three: James 1:17 (Seek justice)

Day Four: Mathew 5:10-12 (Blessed are the persecuted)

Day Five: Romans 7:15 (Doing the things you hate)

Day Six: 2 Chronicles 15:7 (Do not be weak)

Day Seven: 1 John 3:7(Practice righteousness)

⁹"Then you will understand what is right, just, and fair, and you will find the right way to go. ¹⁰ For wisdom will enter your heart, and knowledge will fill you with joy."
Proverbs 2:9-10

Have you ever wondered what is just, fair, and right in life? You can find all the answers to those questions in the Bible and by staying close to God in your life. Whenever you wonder about these things, put them in prayer. Ask God to give you wisdom in your life. Through knowing God, you will know what is good, right, fair, and just. You also know the difference between right and wrong because you were taught the difference at a young age. By reading God's word every day, you will know a lot more than you ever expected to. It opens your eyes to new possibilities.

When you ask for wisdom, believe that you have received it. Also, believe that you will receive it in His timing and in His way. When He knows the timing is right, He will give you the wisdom you asked for. If He sees you needing wisdom about which path to take in your life, whether you need wisdom about a career change, pursuing a relationship with a friend, or going back to school, God will grant you the wisdom you need to be able to make those decisions. Trust in Him. He knows exactly what wisdom you need, and He will give it to you at exactly the right time.

Think back to times when you did things right in your life. Doing things in the right way filled your heart with peace and happiness. Doing the right things for yourself and others often feels so much better than doing the wrong things.

Whenever you are caught up doing the wrong things in your life, you may feel that sick feeling in the pit of your stomach. That's the guilt and shame weighing on your inner conscience. The Holy Spirit and the Lord allow that guilt and shame to come upon your mind, soul, and your heart to teach you exactly how it feels when you do something wrong. They both let that shameful feeling come upon you to show you that you shouldn't sin.

Doing something nice for someone helped the other person feel good. It also made you feel good. The same feeling comes upon you when you do things right, just, and pleasing to God. God smiles on you whenever you do right for someone else and whenever you make the right decisions for yourself.

Letting God have complete control over every aspect of your life gives you so much freedom. Going through all of those emotions helped make you even more grateful for the good times that God has allowed you to have. Letting go of all anger, bitterness, rage, and disappointments freed you from an emotional collapse. Bring free from all of those emotions helped you become a better person.

God knew exactly when you needed to let go of all of those emotions, and He helped you work through them, one by one. Once you learn how to lean on God and ask Him to give you wisdom and knowledge, He will allow you to tap into His knowledge in ways that only He can. He can show you exactly where you need to be in your life. If you ask God to guide you in all of your ways, He will fill your heart, soul, and your mind with His peace that surpasses all human understanding as you walk through life.

PRACTICAL APPLICATIONS:

How have you asked God for wisdom to know what's right, just, and fair in life?

_____

_____

_____

_____

_____

_____

_____

_____

_____

ENGAGE YOUR MIND:

Do you know what is right, just, and fair in your life because of God revealing it to you, or are you going through those questions in your power? Do you truly believe that all wisdom comes from God?

_____

_____

_____

_____

_____

_____

_____

_____

ENGAGE YOUR HEART:

How can you humbly come before God and ask Him for wisdom? What has God revealed to you about the things that are right, just, and fair in your life?

_____
_____
_____
_____
_____
_____
_____
_____
_____
_____

How did He help you gain that type of wisdom?

_____
_____
_____
_____
_____
_____
_____
_____
_____
_____

Week 16

EMBRACE GOD'S DISCIPLINE

SCRIPTURE READINGS:

Day One: Hebrews 12:11 (Be trained by God's discipline)

Day Two: Proverbs 12:1 (Love correction)

Day Three: Proverbs 13:24 (Discipline children)

Day Four: 1 Corinthians 9:27 (Discipline my body)

Day Five: Revelation 3:19 (Repent)

Day Six: Titus 1:8 (Be disciplined)

Day Seven: Proverbs 25:28 (Have self-control)

"My child, don't reject the Lord's discipline, and don't be upset when he corrects you. ¹² *For the Lord corrects those he loves, just as a father corrects a child in whom he delights." Proverbs 3:11-12*

Think back to when you were a kid, and you got corrected, disciplined, and grounded by your dad because you disobeyed him. He was only trying to teach you the difference between right and wrong. He was also trying to help you know how to handle situations better. He also wanted to teach you important lessons about what happens when you disobey God. Your dad might have been saying these things in a way that made you want to mouth off to him in mean ways, or he could have made you shut down in front of him altogether, or his words made you cry. Who knows, maybe you felt all of those emotions rising inside you when he tried to correct you.

However, your father was just trying to protect you from more heartache and more pain later in life. He wanted to teach you lessons that you wouldn't ever forget. He didn't want you to get hurt physically, mentally, or even emotionally by continuing to let you do the wrong things in your life. He wanted to teach you the consequences of every decision. He also wanted to instill wisdom in your heart that every action has an equal and opposite reaction. He didn't want to come down on you hard, but sometimes he probably felt as though you left him no other choice. He had to come down on you harder at certain times just so you would understand. He loves you and wants only the best for you.

You probably didn't like being corrected, especially when you were a teenager. The last thing you thought you needed was your dad yelling at you and scolding you for different reasons. You can also feel that same way whenever God tries to teach you about something or tries to help you correct your behavior. Whenever your dad would try to teach you something, you probably thought, "Oh come on, dad. I know this already. I don't need this lesson again. You're wasting your time!" Nevertheless, your dad still took the time to teach you things over and over again, whether you ever fully grasped his lessons or not. Instead of being annoyed at his teachings, you learned to embrace his teachings and love for you.

That is the same way you react to God when He tries to teach you something important in your life as you get older. You constantly shrug it off, saying, "Oh come on, Lord! I know this already. I don't need that nudge from the Holy Spirit telling me what is right or wrong." God also comes before you with the heart of a concerned parent. He loves you as His child and wants to teach you the best way to go through your life. Rather than get annoyed by His teachings, embrace them, so you know how to better handle your life. Embrace both your dad's teachings and God's teachings with thankfulness. Be willing to learn what they teach you.

PRACTICAL APPLICATION:

In what ways have you rejected the Lord's discipline?

_____

_____

_____

_____

_____

_____

Have you ever been upset over God trying to correct you?

_____

_____

_____

_____

_____

_____

ENGAGE YOUR MIND:

How can you change your thinking to accept the Lord's discipline whenever He tries to give it to you?

_____

_____

_____

_____

_____

_____

How can you tell yourself not to get upset whenever God or someone else in your life tries to correct you or give you advice?

_____

_____

_____

_____

_____

_____

How can you remind yourself not to speak out against any advice that your earthly father gives you, even when you think you know better than he does?

_____

_____

_____

_____

_____

_____

ENGAGE YOUR HEART:

How does it feel to readily accept Godly wisdom and correction from people in your life, such as your parents, boyfriend or husband, or friends?

_____

_____

_____

_____

_____

How do you feel that God loves you and wants to help you know what is right and wrong, so you don't keep making the same mistakes? How do you feel coming before God after you've made mistakes?

_____

_____

_____

_____

_____

Week 17

BE A WISE WOMAN

SCRIPTURE READINGS:

Day One: Proverbs 31:26 (Teachings of kindness)

Day Two: Proverbs 14:1 (Build up her household)

Day Three: Proverbs 12:4 (Crown of her husband)

Day Four: Ephesians 5:22-24 (Submit to your husbands)

Day Five: 1 Timothy 3:2 (Be sober minded)

Day Six: 1 Peter 3:5-6 (Holy women)

Day Seven: Colossians 3:18 (Submit to your husbands)

"A wise woman builds her home, but a foolish woman tears it down with her own hands." Proverbs 14:1

Have you ever wondered what it takes to be a wise woman? It takes courage, discipline, fortitude, love, and patience. Just as it says in this scripture, a wise woman builds her home and makes it strong. But a foolish woman tears her own house down with her own hands. A wise woman fills her house with love, sound biblical teachings, and has patience in every area of her life. She teaches her children about the love of the Lord and the blessings of knowing the Lord on a deep, personal level. She tries her best to get along with her husband and honor him with good communication, even during tough times and difficult subjects. She takes the lessons her parents taught her and teaches them to her kids, friends, and family in the way she knows best. She works through disagreements between her and her husband, and she prays to God for His insight on how to handle tough situations. She prays for and with her kids that they make God-pleasing decisions throughout their lives.

Even though she will fail at all of these things at one time or another, God smiles upon her when she tries her hardest. God helps her become wise as each day goes on. In every circumstance, she gains His knowledge about her life. She readily accepts new teachings from anyone and tries to understand how everyone feels. She tries to respect everyone's different points of view. She embraces God's teachings over her life and readily accepts His wisdom. She builds up her children and encourages them. She lets the little things go instead of getting angry. She sees where she went wrong and apologizes.

On the other hand, a foolish woman doesn't raise her kids in the way of the Lord. She doesn't take into account how important God's word is in her life, her kids' lives, or in her husband's life. She doesn't want to better herself in everything she does because she already thinks she knows everything that she needs to know. She doesn't teach her kids about God or pray for them to know Him on a deeply personal level. She doesn't encourage her kids to follow their dreams, and she doesn't pray with them over their future. Whenever someone tries to teach her or correct her, she gets angry with them instead of understanding their point of view. She single-handedly can ruin her household and cause her marriage to collapse when she doesn't try to work through difficulties with her husband. She causes strife in her household instead of creating harmony. She scoffs at her kids' points of view and laughs at them. She doesn't accept God's way of teaching her things. She tears down her marriage without realizing it until it's too late; she tears down her children, and they, in turn, walk away from her. She is angry at the little things and doesn't apologize. Take the time to reexamine your life and figure out which woman you would rather be.

PRACTICAL APPLICATIONS:

You can ask yourself, "Which woman am I?" In what ways are you like the wise woman or the foolish woman?

_____

_____

_____

_____

_____

What would you rather be: a woman who builds her household up in the Lord or a woman who tears her house down by never doing the right things?

_____

_____

_____

_____

_____

ENGAGE YOUR MIND:

How can you change your thinking to want to be the wiser woman instead of thinking you know everything like the foolish woman?

_____

_____

_____

_____

_____

In what ways can you turn away from being the foolish woman and make yourself a wiser woman who cherishes her household and the way she raises her family?

_____

_____

_____

_____

_____

ENGAGE YOUR HEART:

In what ways can you build yourself, your family, and your household up like the wise woman?

_____
_____
_____
_____
_____
_____

What was your reaction to realizing that you can stop acting like the foolish woman?

_____
_____
_____
_____
_____

How did it feel when God opened your eyes to the ways you were the foolish woman?

_____
_____
_____
_____
_____

Week 18

A TIME FOR EVERYTHING

SCRIPTURE READING:

Day One: Habakkuk 2:3 (Appointed time)

Day Two: Ecclesiastes 8:6 (A way for everything)

Day Three: Psalm 27:4 (Wait for the Lord)

Day Four: Galatians 6:9 (Do not give up)

Day Five: Proverbs 3:5-6 (Trust in the Lord)

Day Six: Ecclesiastes 3:11 (Everything beautiful)

Day Seven: Lamentations 3:25-26 (Wait for the Lord)

"For everything there is a season, a time for every activity under heaven."
Ecclesiastes 3:1

If you have ever wondered why things happen the way they do, there is a reason for everything. However, it's not just a reason -- it's God's reason. He could have been protecting you from serious harm or a serious accident by having an ice or snow storm come over your city. He could have protected you by not having your car start to keep you from driving. When you were out partying and had a bit too much to drink, He could have had a friend offer to drive you home so you wouldn't drive drunk. He could have had you in the middle of an accident scene because you're a first responder or a nurse who needed to help out a victim. He could have kept you from walking across the street at the same crosswalk that you use every day because He knew a car would run the red light. He could have kept you from gossiping about someone else to protect your friendship with that person.

He could have kept your husband from going on the business trip that he was planning to go on so you two could work out some problems in your marriage. He could have kept your daughter home from school or practice for a game because He knew there was a medical diagnosis that you needed to uncover before it was too late. You could've gotten home minutes before a huge storm hit, whispering a prayer in awe of how good God is and how fast He works things out in your favor.

God also could have been protecting you from danger or physical harm by getting you out of a situation where a friend was about to drive when they were under the influence. God could have also been protecting you for many years by not letting you hear or see the verbal and emotional abuse between people in your family. He could have also been protecting you by helping you gain wisdom about the relationship you're in with your boyfriend. He could have helped you get out of that relationship before it caused you any more harm or even killed you.

If someone in your life dies because of his or her foolish choices, yet you live, that is not God's curse on you. That is God's blessing on you. That is God still saying to you, "I still have a purpose for your life, and I want you to fulfill it." If someone in your life is mourning because they lost someone they love, that is God's invitation for you to just be present with them in that situation. God wants you to be there for them in His ways. He wants you to show His love to your friend who is suffering. That circumstance could be God telling you to be there for your friend in ways that only you can do through Him. If someone starts losing their faith in God, that could be your cue from God to step in and try to steer them back towards a life of faith. Whether you realize certain things that happen are God's protection or not. He is always with you in the middle of every situation.

PRACTICAL APPLICATIONS:

What changes do you need to make in your life to accept God's holy protection?

_____

_____

_____

_____

_____

_____

_____

_____

Have you ever had a near-death experience and realized it was God's holy protection over you?

_____

_____

_____

_____

_____

_____

_____

ENGAGE YOUR MIND:

Has your faith ever been shaken because of your circumstances? How can you change your thinking to trust in God's protection over your life?

_____

_____

_____

_____

_____

_____

How did God help you realize that everything happens for His reason and His reason alone?

_____
_____
_____
_____
_____
_____

How did you feel when God spoke to you about His protection?

_____
_____
_____
_____
_____

In what ways did He help you realize that everything happens for His reason? How did it feel knowing that everything happens for His reason?

_____
_____
_____
_____
_____

Week 19

ENJOY LIFE

SCRIPTURE READINGS:

Day One: Proverbs 17:22 (Cheerful heart)

Day Two: Ecclesiastes 5:18 (Find enjoyment in toil)

Day Three: Ecclesiastes 2:24 (Find enjoyment in work)

Day Four: Ecclesiastes 11:9 (Cheer the days of youth)

Day Five: John 16:24 (Ask and you shall receive)

Day Six: Psalm 16:11 (Make known the path of life)

Day Seven: Luke 1:47 (Rejoice in God)

"Yet God has made everything beautiful for its own time. He has planted eternity in the human heart, but even so, people cannot see the whole scope of God's work from beginning to end. ¹² So I concluded there is nothing better than to be happy and enjoy ourselves as long as we can." Ecclesiastes 3: 11-12

Everyday life can get exhausting for you, no matter how much you may balance your workload. From work responsibilities and family obligations to figuring out how and when you will get free time for yourself, life can be overwhelming. If you choose to let it, pretty much anything in your life can overwhelm you. You have to choose what you want to put your thoughts into and how you will let your thoughts control your life.

It says in this Bible passage that God has placed eternity in the human heart, but even so, people can't see the whole scope of God from beginning to end. You are only human, and you will not understand why things happen the way they do, and a lot of the time, you're not supposed to understand why things happen. Only God understands those things. His knowledge is beyond your understanding because He is God, and you're only human. It's okay to ask God for clarification. There are many times where you can pray about things and then give up your thoughts to God by saying, "Lord, I trust that you will get me through this situation with your power. Help me to be ok with not understanding everything the way you understand it. Fill me with your peace and comfort. Help me to accept your ways over my ways. Thank you that you know how everything will work out. Thank you that you made everything beautiful in its own time. Thank you that I'll never understand things the way you understand them."

Take heart. There is hope for those of you who feel overwhelmed. No matter how you feel, remember that everything has a purpose in your life. Every hard time has its place in your life. Every hard time teaches you how to react and how not to react. Every hard time helps you become a stronger and wiser woman. Start telling yourself that there is still so much to be thankful for, no matter how difficult things are in the present moment. Look for the beauty in each day and find something to be thankful for, even if you're struggling. Instead of automatically giving in to despair, think about the many blessings that God has given you in your life.

You are breathing. You're able to provide for your family and able to help your kids with schoolwork. You're never hungry, and you always have enough to eat. You're able to help others get through hard times by inspiring them to not give up. You have eternity waiting for you when you get to Heaven. There is nothing better than to try to be as happy as you can on earth and to enjoy every part of your life, even though some days will be harder than others.

Once you learn to enjoy things in your life, everything will be easier to get through. You will find more joy, peace of mind and be able to think clearer even in uncertain situations. You will be able to name your blessings and cherish the good times. God wants you to experience good times, and He wants you to experience the true joys that this life brings. He also wants you to trust in His timing and His plans for your life. Tell yourself that no matter what life throws at you, you're going to enjoy life to the fullest.

PRACTICAL APPLICATIONS:

In what ways can you enjoy your life to the fullest?

_____
_____
_____
_____
_____
_____

In what areas of your life do you struggle to find joy each day?

_____
_____
_____
_____
_____
_____

What makes it hard to find joy in your life?

_____
_____
_____
_____
_____
_____

Why is it hard for you to see blessings among the hardships of life?

_____
_____
_____
_____
_____
_____

ENGAGE YOUR MIND:

What can you do to change your thinking around and view every day as a blessing?

_____
_____
_____
_____
_____
_____

What kind of changes do you have to make mentally for you to see that each day and every circumstance is a blessing?

_____
_____
_____
_____
_____

ENGAGE YOUR HEART:

How does it feel embracing every day as a blessing, no matter what is happening?

_____
_____
_____
_____
_____

Week 20

DO NOT BRAG

SCRIPTURE READINGS:

Day One: Mathew 6:1 (Don't practice unrighteousness)

Day Two: Jeremiah 9:23 (Do not boast about wisdom)

Day Three: Proverbs 27:1 (Don't boast about tomorrow)

Day Four: 1 Corinthians 1:31 (Boast in the Lord)

Day Five: Galatians 6:14 (Boast in the cross)

Day Six: James 4:16 (Don't boast in arrogance)

Day Seven: Proverbs 11:2 (Be humble and obtain wisdom)

"2 Don't make rash promises, and don't be hasty in bringing matters before God. After all, God is in heaven, and you are here on earth. So, let your words be few."
Ecclesiastes 5:2

Have you ever been tempted to speak out in a situation that didn't concern you? How about making promises to a friend or family member that you didn't intend to keep? Have you ever been in a hurry to lay your feelings at God's feet, begging Him to take them? This Bible verse says not to make rash promises and to not bring matters before God in a hurry.

You can always bring your prayers, petitions, and concerns before God, but you don't have to bring them in front of God in a hurried manner. Remember, God sees all and knows all already, so He knows exactly what is on your mind before you even utter a word. God is in Heaven, and you are on earth. He knows how to handle every situation. Pray for wisdom to be able to know when to speak and when not to speak, whether it's at work, in your family, or any other place.

God doesn't want you to make promises that you don't intend to keep. He doesn't want your prayers to be quick and then for you to go back to your day. Rather, He wants you to spend time with Him. He wants to get to know you better. He wants a personal relationship with you. If something is bothering you, take time to pray about it. Think about your prayers. Think about each word you are saying in each prayer. Enjoy praying because it will only bring you and God that much closer together.

Whenever you are in situations where you're tempted to speak out, remember to let your words be few. It can be very difficult to keep your mouth shut, especially if you feel you need to speak out. Whenever you're tempted to speak out at work, think about how your words could affect your job. If you speak out at the wrong times, you could end up losing your job. You could also be known as a big mouth around the office if you make your opinions known too much. You could end up hurting someone's reputation if you choose to engage in office gossip.

If you speak out too much in your marriage, or if you complain too much, your husband may not want to open up to you. He may start avoiding you all together so that he doesn't have to feel emasculated or manipulated by you. Think about how your words can affect your marriage before you just start mouthing off—approach important subjects with a calm spirit. Only approach your husband on tough topics when your mind is right. If you or your husband is not in a calm frame of mind, then wait to talk to him. Approach him with love and sincerity.

Whenever you feel you need to address certain things with your kids, do so with a calm spirit instead of an accusing tone in your voice. If you constantly find fault with your kids and constantly critique them, they will shy away from you and avoid you. But if you can approach them with love in your heart and teach them important things in life with love, they will embrace you and your teachings. Approach every conversation with your kids with love.

In all of these situations, it is important to let your words be few so that you don't say the wrong things and make bad situations worse. Let God guide your words in every situation.

PRACTICAL APPLICATIONS:

In what areas of your life has God told you that you need to speak less? How can you remind yourself to let your words be few?

_____

_____

_____

_____

_____

_____

_____

_____

In what ways has God helped you speak less? How does it feel to speak less and listen more?

_____

_____

_____

_____

_____

_____

_____

_____

How can you willingly surrender your need to speak out or be heard over to God?

_____

_____

_____

_____

_____

_____

_____

_____

ENGAGE YOUR MIND:

How can you change your mind to speak less and listen more in every situation?

_____
_____
_____
_____
_____
_____
_____
_____
_____
_____

ENGAGE YOUR HEART:

How does it feel to let your words be few and listen more?

_____
_____
_____
_____
_____
_____
_____
_____
_____

Week 21

BURDENS

SCRIPTURE READINGS:

Day One: Mathew 11:28-30 (His burden is light)

Day Two: Psalm 55:22 (Cast burdens on God)

Day Three: Galatians 6:2 (Bear one another's burdens)

Day Four: Acts 20:35 (Help the weak)

Day Five: Jeremiah 23:36 (Prophecy from the Lord)

Day Six: Galatians 6:5 (Bear your own load)

Day Seven: Psalm 68:19 (God bears us up)

"For you will break the yoke of their slavery and lift the heavy burden from their shoulders." Isaiah 9:4

Have you ever felt the burdens of life were never going to end? Think for a minute about the things that burden you. Maybe it's the weight of the tasks you have to do at work, at home, taking care of your family, kids, or paying bills. Maybe it's finding a balance in your work and your home. When was the last time that you had a date night with your husband or did something fun as a family besides playing board games or watching television?

If you need a break, take everything that's on your mind before God. He wants to help you find rest and for you to enjoy your life. If you're feeling constantly burdened by your everyday life, think about why you're feeling burdened. Think of ways that you can take away some of that stress. If you're feeling stressed out because of work, talk to your boss or coworkers about taking some of the workloads off of your shoulders. See what they say, and if they are willing to help you, take them up on their offers. Keep doing your work to the best of your ability, and ask God to help you remember to only do one task and one assignment at a time.

If you're stressing out in your home life with your kids, take the time to ask for your family's help with taking care of them. See if your family members (whether it's your mom, dad, sister, brother, or your extended family) would be willing to take care of the kids for the day, the weekend, or even just to watch them for the afternoon until you get home from work. It is perfectly okay to ask your family members for help if you ever start feeling like you're overwhelmed.

If you find that you're struggling with your marriage, make sure you talk to God about it first and foremost. Ask Him to reveal where you and your husband are struggling, and talk to your husband about it calmly. Explain to him how you feel and how you think you both are struggling. If you both feel the need to go to counseling, and God is leading you to go to counseling to help your marriage, then, by all means, do it. Make the time to talk to each other. Pray for one another. Start praying with each other again too. See how doing those things improves your marriage.

God wants to break every chain and take every burden from you. He wants to take every burden off of your shoulders in ways that only He can. Let Him step in and work in your life in ways that you never expected Him to. Let Him work on and in your marriage. Let Him help you reconnect to your husband. Let Him take the stress off of you in your work life by providing more time to do tasks. Let Him work in your interactions with your kids. Ask Him to be with you every time you talk to your kids and help your conversations be calmer and filled with love. Get into the habit of asking Him to take any burdens off of your shoulders. In every area of your life, He can and will take away the burdens you're dealing with.

PRACTICAL APPLICATIONS:

In what areas of your life do you need God to remove the burden from your shoulders?

_____

_____

_____

_____

_____

_____

Have you asked Him for help with managing your stress?

_____

_____

_____

_____

_____

ENGAGE YOUR MIND:

In what ways have you asked God to help you bring a work and life balance into your everyday life?

_____

_____

_____

_____

_____

What areas of your mind need a much-needed break?

_____

_____

_____

_____

_____

ENGAGE YOUR HEART:

How does it feel to change your view of burdens into lessons that you can learn?

_____

_____

_____

_____

_____

_____

How can you remind yourself to lay any burdens that are on your mind and heart before God?

_____

_____

_____

_____

_____

_____

How does it feel when God lifts burdens off of your shoulders?

_____

_____

_____

_____

_____

_____

Week 22

BOAST ABOUT CHRIST

SCRIPTURE READINGS:

Day One: Jeremiah 9:23 (Don't boast in wisdom)

Day Two: Proverbs 27:1 (Do not boast about tomorrow)

Day Three: 1 Corinthians 4:7 (Everything is a gift)

Day Four: Psalm 94:4 (All evildoers boast)

Day Five: 2 Corinthians 11:30 (Boast of my weakness)

Day Six: James 3:5 (the tongue boasts of great things)

Day Seven: 1 Corinthians 1:31 (Boast in the Lord)

"But those who wish to boast should boast in this alone: that they truly know me and understand that I am the Lord who demonstrates unfailing love and who brings justice and righteousness to the earth, and that I delight in these things. I, the Lord, have spoken!" Jeremiah 9:24

What things do you boast about? Do you boast in your love for your kids, about your husband, your good job, your nice house, your great extended family? Do you boast about how well your kids are doing in school? Do you boast about how blessed you are by God with everything you have, or do you completely forget how good God is to you? A lot of the time, when you brag, you end up thinking that everything that you have isn't a blessing. You might start thinking that everything is done by your work and by pure luck. On the contrary, blessings are not in your life by pure luck. God gives them all to you.

You can change your mindset to go from boasting about the way things are going in your life to only boasting about God, your love for Him, and boasting about how He has impacted and saved your life. If you can learn to focus your boasting on God and how amazing He is, you will see more and more beauty in the world around you. You will be able to notice things you used to take for granted, such as getting to work and back home safely every day, and you will cherish the days that you can work from home.

Making your family dinner every night can also be seen as a blessing. The downtime you get every night after work to do something other than your work tasks can be seen as a nice refresher instead of being seen as a burden. You will complain less about your circumstances and see each one as a learning process, and you will also see each one as a stepping-stone onto bigger and better things. Instead of feeling burdened when you have to help your kids with their schoolwork, you can start seeing it as a privilege and an honor to help your kids succeed.

In your marriage, you can see every interaction with your husband as a way to show Christ's love. If you can learn to approach him with kindness and love in your heart, just as God approaches you with love in His heart, you will find that your discussions about any topic are going to be filled with kindness, compassion, and love. Make the time each day to pray for and with each other, and make faith something you both want to teach your kids about. Show love to one another, so your kids know how to show love to others around them.

Instead of making God the last person you boast about in your life, make Him the first person you boast about. Boast about how knowing Him on a deeply personal level has changed your life, heart, and your mindset for the better. Brag about how God has changed your views about life and about how you see each day as a blessing and as a new opportunity to learn and grow.

Delight in telling others about Him and the free grace and mercy that He wants to give to everyone. Help others want to come to know Jesus as their personal Lord and Savior. Don't be afraid to tell others how they can receive forgiveness from their sins if they just come before Him and ask for it. Boast about how much you love God and how every blessing comes from Him. Tell others about how He has delivered you from the injustices of this world and how He can do the same things for them if they just call on His name and ask Him. Be willing to boast about His never-ending mercies.

PRACTICAL APPLICATIONS:

Have you boasted about God in your life lately?

_____
_____
_____
_____
_____
_____
_____
_____
_____
_____
_____
_____

How can you boast about what God has done for you?

_____
_____
_____
_____
_____
_____
_____
_____
_____
_____
_____
_____
_____
_____
_____
_____

ENGAGE YOUR MIND:

How can you change your mindset to want to boast about the goodness of God in your life instead of complaining about your circumstances?

_____
_____
_____
_____
_____
_____
_____
_____
_____
_____
_____

ENGAGE YOUR HEART:

How do you feel when you boast about God's love?

_____
_____
_____
_____
_____
_____
_____
_____
_____

Week 23

MERCY OF GOD

SCRIPTURE READINGS:

Day One: Hebrews 4:16 (Obtain mercy)

Day Two: Ephesians 2:4-5 (Rich in mercy)

Day Three: Luke 6:36 (Be merciful)

Day Four: James 2:13 (Mercy triumphs over judgement)

Day Five: Mathew 5:7 (Blessed are the merciful)

Day Six: Titus 3:5 (According to His mercy)

Day Seven: Psalm 145:9 (His mercy is everywhere)

"The faithful love of the Lord never ends! His mercies never cease.[23] Great is his faithfulness; his mercies begin afresh each morning.[24] I say to myself, "The Lord is my inheritance; therefore, I will hope in him! "Lamentations 3:22-24

God's mercies never cease. They are never-ending. But sometimes, it is hard to see every circumstance as a blessing. Sometimes, it is difficult to see hard times as lessons given to you by God to strengthen you as a woman. The hard times were and always will be meant to strengthen your mind, soul, and heart and strengthen you physically. When you thought you couldn't go on in your life is when God showed His love and mercy to you by carrying you when you couldn't walk.

Other mercies from God include times when you were spared from being in an accident on the road or the times when you were given a break when you needed it the most, whether it was in the form of taking time off from work or taking a vacation by yourself or time with your family. His mercies are new every morning, and they include everything from waking you up every day, your ability to walk, talk, think, breathe, and be able to do your job well. You can do your job at work to the best of your ability because of Him. You come home from work every day, grateful for the fact that you have a home to come back to.

God is faithful in everything that you do in your life. Think back to a time when He helped you through a difficult situation at work. He brought you through that time and helped you understand more about the company you work for, and He helped you understand more about yourself as a person. He has also helped you through any troubles that you have with your marriage. He gives you the right words to say to your husband at the right time. He allows you to talk to each other in ways that only He can.

The Lord's faithfulness never ends, and it never will end. If you can begin to see His faithfulness in every area of your life, you will see blessings where there used to be hardships at every turn. You will see each hard time as a learning process. You will see the beauty and God's goodness in your life, even among the storms of life. You will appreciate everything in your life all that much more. Whenever you have a hard day, remind yourself of this Bible verse that His faithfulness never ends and that His mercies are new every morning. Remind yourself that the hard times will and do pass and that each day has enough trouble of its own.

Do not be hard on yourself or ever think that you're going through the rough times in life alone. God is always with you every step of the way. Each new day is a chance to give yourself to God. Each new day you can remind yourself to trust in God and to trust in yourself. This is how you can and will get through any task at work, at home, or with your kids -- even if the task in front of you seems daunting.

Each new day is an opportunity to boast about how good God is in your life. You are saved by God's mercy and grace. You are forgiven by Him every day for your sins. Learn to put your hope in Him no matter what may be going on. If you constantly trust in Him, things in life will be that much easier to get through. Embrace His mercies and His faithfulness every day, and be thankful that they both never cease.

PRACTICAL APPLICATION:

How can you teach yourself to see everything in your life as the Lord's blessings?

_____
_____
_____
_____
_____

What is one act of faith you showed God today, demonstrating you trust Him?

_____
_____
_____
_____
_____

ENGAGE YOUR MIND:

How have you reminded yourself to rest in God's mercies every day?

_____
_____
_____
_____
_____

In what ways has He revealed His faithfulness to you in life?

_____
_____
_____
_____
_____

ENGAGE YOUR HEART:

How do you feel when God reveals His mercies to you in your everyday situations?

_____
_____
_____
_____
_____
_____
_____
_____
_____

How do you feel when you rely on the mercy of God?

_____
_____
_____
_____
_____
_____
_____
_____
_____

Week 24

STARK WARNINGS

SCRIPTURE READINGS:

Day One: 2 Timothy 2:13 (He is faithful)

Day Two: Deuteronomy 7:9 (God is faithful)

Day Three: 1 John 1:9 (Cleansed from unrighteousness)

Day Four: Psalm 33:4 (His word is true)

Day Five: Psalm 86:15 (Steadfast faithfulness)

Day Six: Proverbs 28:20 (Abound in blessings)

Day Seven: Psalm 89:8 (Faithfulness all around)

"Have you seen this, son of man?" he asked. "Is it nothing to the people of Judah that they commit these detestable sins, leading the whole nation into violence, thumbing their noses at me, and provoking my anger? [18] Therefore, I will respond in fury. I will neither pity nor spare them. And though they cry for mercy, I will not listen." Ezekiel 8:17-18

Every person on earth commits detestable sins in their life. Some people will see the errors of their ways and ask God for forgiveness, while others will never repent. In this lesson, the people of Judah were committing detestable sins and leading their entire nation into violence. God gave them a stark warning about what would happen to them if they kept provoking His anger. He then said He would respond in a fury, and He wouldn't pity or spare them if they continued to act like that. Even if the people of Judah cried out to Him for mercy, He wouldn't listen to their cries.

He is asking you if you have seen the detestable things people have done. No doubt you have seen some pretty horrible things in your life, whether they have been things at work, things that are reported on the news, or something bad that happened to an extended family member. Mercifully, you may not have even been directly involved with any of them. Take the horrible and detestable things that you have seen and heard in your life and use them as learning experiences as to how not to act. Remember, God sees, hears, and knows everything, so He knows when, where, why, and how bad things will happen. Whenever you see bad things happening in your town, your neighborhood, or your home, if you can step in safely to stop those bad things from happening, then God wants you to step in.

He is also asking you to search your heart and think about all of the wrong things that you have done in your life. No one can get away from sin, and everyone sins every day, even though they might do their best not to sin. Think of the things that you have done wrong in your life. You have lost your temper towards your kids, your husband, and your extended family. You have probably mouthed off at work from time to time. You have probably gossiped in the office about a coworker. You have probably vented to friends about how your husband doesn't do everything you request him to do on any given day. Have you ever wanted to get even with someone who mistreated you or pay them back in an even meaner way than they hurt you? All of those instances are where you completely lost touch with God, and instead, you let Satan control your mind, control your thinking, and even let him have complete control over your actions.

Satan makes you think that acting irrationally or meanly towards someone is not a bad thing to do. Satan makes you think that it is completely okay to act that way towards other people and not care how your words and actions may affect you or how your words and actions affect other people. He doesn't want you to think twice about the bad things you or other people are doing. Rather, Satan wants you to continue turning a blind eye and continue turning deaf ears to the bad things happening in this world. Satan doesn't want you telling people to repent of their sins and ask for forgiveness before it becomes too late.

God doesn't like when you judge other people, act out in anger towards other people, or engage in gossip towards others. He wants you to take the words in this scripture to heart and remind yourself that He could just as easily be talking about how He could react towards the detestable things you have done in your life.

PRACTICAL APPLICATION:

How can you stop bad things from happening?

_____

_____

_____

_____

_____

_____

_____

What detestable things have you done in your life? Have you asked God for forgiveness from them?

_____

_____

_____

_____

_____

_____

_____

ENGAGE YOUR MIND:

How can you change your way of thinking and stop thinking bad thoughts?

_____

_____

_____

_____

_____

_____

How has God put it on your heart to speak out when you see bad things happening?

_____
_____
_____
_____
_____
_____
_____
_____
_____
_____

ENGAGE YOUR HEART:

How does it feel to speak out against bad or cruel situations in life?

_____
_____
_____
_____
_____
_____
_____
_____
_____
_____

Week 25

AN UNFAITHFUL WIFE

SCRIPTURE READINGS:

Day One: Proverbs 12:22 (Cheating and lying)

Day Two: Colossians 3:9-10 (Do not lie)

Day Three: Deuteronomy 23:17-18 (Don't be a prostitute)

Day Four: 1 Corinthians 6:9-11 (Sexually immoral)

Day Five: Proverbs 6:24-26 (Price of prostitution)

Day Six: 1 Kings 14:24 (Cult prostitutes)

Day Seven: Leviticus 21:14 (He shall not marry a prostitute)

"I will leave her to die of thirst, as in a dry and barren wilderness.⁴ And I will not love her children, for they were conceived in prostitution.⁵ Their mother is a shameless prostitute and became pregnant in a shameful way." Hosea 2:3-5

An unfaithful wife can easily bring shame to her husband. If a woman so much as looks at another man in a lustful way or thinks that she wants to have sex with him, she is already committing adultery in her heart and mind. If you have ever gotten a divorce because of being unfaithful in your marriage, take a minute to think back to what led to your downfall as a wife. Was it the fact that your then-husband wasn't giving you everything you desired intimately, physically, mentally, financially, emotionally? Did you ever expect to fall into temptation and sleep with another man or even multiple men that weren't your husband? Every woman can fall into temptation with someone who isn't her husband. Being an unfaithful wife can bring shame to your marriage and your life in general.

This Bible lesson goes into detail about what God will do if you're an unfaithful wife. It can seem pretty harsh, but that is the point that God is trying to make. He wants women everywhere to know the consequences if she falls into sin with another man who isn't her husband. He says that He will leave her to die of thirst as if she were in a barren and dry wilderness. He also says He will not love her children if they were conceived in prostitution. He also says that the kid's mother is a shameless prostitute and didn't become pregnant right away; she became pregnant to disgrace her and her offspring. If she had become pregnant with a man whom she was married to and then a child was conceived, then the pregnancy and child would have been conceived in a way that glorifies God. Any woman who sleeps with a man who isn't her husband and gets pregnant doesn't glorify God.

That means that any woman who has children when she isn't married brings shame to herself. She disgraces her kids as well because everyone will know that she had them outside of marriage. No woman ever wants to be labeled as a prostitute, so women everywhere should take God's warnings in this Bible lesson to heart. Always be on your guard against anything that doesn't bring pleasure to God. Keep yourself away from any situation that might spell disaster to your marriage or family. No matter how charming the other man may seem, you can always get yourself out of that type of situation. Ask God for help to resist that type of temptation every time you're presented with it.

It can present itself at any time and anywhere and in many different forms. Whether it's from going out on the town with friends and seeing a guy that you think is cute, or having a few "harmless drinks" with a coworker who just happens to be a guy, or even purposely going out by yourself and leaving your phone at home or in the car so your husband can't contact you. All of those are perfect scenarios for infidelity to happen in a marriage. Be aware of how Satan can be trying to trick you, and ask God to help you stand firm in your vows and your love for your husband. God is always with you through every case of temptation, and the even better news is that He will always help you find a way out of it too.

PRACTICAL APPLICATION:

In what ways have you ever thought about being unfaithful? Have you been unfaithful in your marriage?

_____
_____
_____
_____
_____
_____
_____

Did you ever get tempted to cheat?

_____
_____
_____
_____
_____
_____
_____

In what ways has God gotten you out of a potential cheating situation? Did He help you recognize that cheating is what Satan was trying to trick you into?

_____
_____
_____
_____
_____
_____
_____

ENGAGE YOUR MIND:

In what ways has God helped you remain firm in your vows to your husband?

_____

_____

_____

_____

_____

_____

_____

_____

ENGAGE YOUR HEART:

How did you feel after you thought about or engaged in cheating? Did you ask God for forgiveness?

_____

_____

_____

_____

_____

_____

_____

_____

Week 26

GIVING TO THE NEEDY

SCRIPTURE READINGS:

Day One: 2 Corinthians 9:7 (Give kindly)

Day Two: Mathew 25:35 (Being there for others)

Day Three: Mark 12:41-44 (Giving all)

Day Four: Proverbs 19:17 (Give to the poor)

Day Five: Acts 20:34 (Ministering to necessities)

Day Six: Psalm 104: 28 (Filled with good things)

Day Seven: Mathew 7: 11 (Give good things)

Giving can be a hard thing to do. Whenever you see someone in need, do you want to automatically give them help in any way they need it, or do you walk away from them thinking, "I just don't have the resources or time right now to help this person."? God teaches that you should always do your best to help that person get food, water, and shelter whenever you see someone in need. You never know how hungry they may be or when they had their last meal. Even if it's only giving them a few dollars to get food from a fast-food restaurant or a soup kitchen, it is still better than walking away from them and not helping them. You don't have to give them extravagant amounts of money. If $20 is all you have, and you feel led by the Holy Spirit to give the person money for food or water, then, by all means, follow the Holy Spirit's lead. God will smile on you when you give your last $20 to a person who may need it more than you.

This Bible passage warns you that when you give to someone in need, don't let your right hand know what your left hand is doing. What that means is, do not seek out attention for the things you do for others. Don't give extravagant gifts to anyone and expect things in return for the nice things you did. Don't give big money to the church to be seen as a better Christian. It also means not helping someone if all you expect is for that person to return the favor more extravagantly.

Don't go all over town, in your neighborhood, or even among your family, and start bragging, saying, "I just gave this person my last $20! I'm a better person and a better Christian than those who don't bother to give to the people." Rather than go around bragging like that and thinking that you're better than other people, remember the times when you needed something, and someone helped you out, whether it was by buying you food or a drink. Be humble and remind yourself that you need help at certain times too. So, don't be afraid or too proud to offer someone else help when they need it the most. Who knows, maybe one day, you could be in that very person's position wishing someone would see your circumstances and act humbly towards you. Never be too proud or think that you are better than anyone else who needs help. Everyone needs someone's help at one point or another.

When you tithe in church, give in privacy. No one except you and God need to know how, where, why, and when you gave help to someone in need. If you see someone in need and the Holy Spirit moves you to help that person, don't be afraid to follow God's prompting. You could end up saving someone's life by making that one little gesture of kindness. And as long as you don't go bragging about things you do for other people, then your Father in Heaven will reward you for your goodness towards others. Keep everything that you give, whether it's money, time, talents, or your treasure, in the stillness of your heart -- between you and the Lord. God will always reward you for the nice things you do for your church or anyone in need.

PRACTICAL APPLICATIONS:

Have you ever been tempted to walk away when you saw someone in need? How did God tell you to help anyone in need?

_____

_____

_____

_____

_____

_____

_____

_____

_____

_____

_____

ENGAGE YOUR MIND:

How did God change your mindset from "How can helping this person benefit me?" to "How can I make this person's life better?"

_____

_____

_____

_____

_____

_____

_____

_____

_____

_____

_____

Are you more willing to give to others around you out of the goodness of your heart, or do you struggle with giving to others?

_____
_____
_____
_____
_____
_____
_____
_____
_____
_____

ENGAGE YOUR HEART:

How do you feel about helping others out of the goodness of your heart, even if you have nothing?

_____
_____
_____
_____
_____
_____
_____
_____
_____
_____

Week 27

INNER PURITY

SCRIPTURE READINGS:

Day One: Mathew 5:8 (Pure in heart)

Day Two: Psalm 119:9 (Keep His ways pure)

Day Three: Psalm 51:10 (Renew a right spirit)

Day Four: Colossians 3:5 (Put to death impurity)

Day Five: Romans 13:14 (Do not gratify the flesh)

Day Six: Philippians 4:8 (Whatever is pure)

Day Seven: James 4:8 (Pure at heart)

"Then Jesus called to the crowd to come and hear. "All of you listen," he said, "and try to understand. [15] It's not what goes into your body that defiles you; you are defiled by what comes from your heart." Mark 7:14-15

J esus was the preacher of all preachers and the teacher of all teachers. He never sinned, never made a mistake, and always did what His Father asked of Him. In this Bible passage, He called the people around Him to listen to His teachings and begging them to understand what He was saying. He told them that it's not what goes into a person's body that defiles them. But that a person is defiled by what comes out of their mouths and by the words and thoughts that come from their heart.

This means it's not the things you eat that can make you sick. Rather it is the things you say, do, and how you act towards situations that defile your life. If you are constantly angry over things in your work life or your home life, you have to stop and ask yourself why things have you so uptight and angry. Once you identify why you are so worked up and so angry, you have to work to eliminate the cause of that type of stress. Ask God to change your viewpoint from "These things will always stress me out" to "This situation too shall pass. I am a bigger person when I don't get as angry or worked up."

If you are constantly stressed out at home, ask yourself why you feel that way. Then talk to your husband and maybe even your kids about the way you are feeling. The people in your life will only know about how you are struggling if you choose to tell them. If you are struggling in your personal life as a Christian, talk to someone about it, whether it is your husband, a trusted friend, a counselor, or even a pastor. Telling someone, anyone, about the way you are struggling is the first step in admitting that you have a problem. It is the first step in getting yourself the help you need.

If you are struggling with anger and constantly find yourself swearing either in your mind, out loud, or even under your breath, you have to remind yourself that swearing is in itself a sin. Even if it feels good to let off steam and to swear when you're going through a hard time, it still is a very difficult habit to break once you start doing it. Ask God to come into your heart and to forgive you for swearing all the time. You can even ask Him to start making you feel guilty when you swear. That way, you get it through your head that you shouldn't be swearing, no matter what situation you're in.

If you are struggling with your self-worth or with finding your purpose, again, talk to someone about it. Most importantly, talk to God about the way you're feeling. Open up to Him about why and how you are struggling. Once you start opening up to people about the areas in which you're struggling, then you can start working on improving your mindset and your life altogether. There is no shame in admitting that you are struggling with things at any time in your life. There is also no shame in crying out to God for help. He wants to remind you that you can come to Him at any time, day or night, with whatever you might be struggling with. Nothing comes as a surprise to God. Ask Him to reveal the areas in your heart, mind, and your life that you need to regain control over, whether it's your thoughts, words, or your actions.

PRACTICAL APPLICATION:

In what ways have you tried to change the way you think, talk, or act?

_____
_____
_____
_____
_____
_____
_____
_____
_____
_____
_____
_____

ENGAGE YOUR MIND:

How has God reminded you that you can come to Him and ask Him to change the way you think every day?

_____
_____
_____
_____
_____
_____
_____
_____
_____
_____
_____
_____

ENGAGE YOUR HEART:

How has it felt when God softened your heart and helped you realize that everything you do and say has a heart effect on your life?

_____
_____
_____
_____
_____
_____
_____
_____
_____
_____
_____
_____
_____
_____
_____
_____
_____
_____
_____
_____
_____
_____

Week 28

DON'T JUDGE

SCRIPTURE READINGS:

Day One: Mathew 7:1-5 (Do not judge)

Day Two: James 4:11-12 (Don't speak evil)

Day Three: Ephesians 4:29 (No corrupting talk)

Day Four: Titus 3:1-2 (Speak evil of no one)

Day Five: Proverbs 31:9 (Judge righteously)

Day Six: Galatians 6:1 (Keep watch)

Day Seven: 2 Corinthians 5:10 (Judgement seat of Christ)

It is important not to judge people; otherwise, you will be judged in that same way. Think back to a time when you started casting judgment on someone else because of how they looked, talked, walked, dressed, worked, or anything else in between. Every person on earth goes through times where they start judging other people for the things they have done or the things they have not done. Every person also goes through times when they condemn another person. If you don't want others casting judgment on you, then you have to do your best not to cast judgment on another person for any reason.

Do not judge a mother by how she raises her kids if it is not the exact way you would raise your kids. Don't talk down to other mothers just because they aren't raising their kids in the same way you are. Don't talk down to or condemn other moms because they aren't raising their kids with the same Christian values that you are raising yours. Don't start criticizing another woman just because she doesn't discipline her kids the same way you discipline your kids.

Don't judge another woman at work for the way she dresses. If there is a specific dress code to be followed and she is not following it, then nicely make her aware of it. Don't go behind her back and rat her out to your boss for breaking the dress code because that could easily start animosity between the two of you. Don't criticize someone else at work for sharing their ideas when you are all in a conference room, trying to brainstorm different ideas about a project. Rather than making a person feel bad about sharing their opinions for a project, make them feel like their opinions matter. Make them feel as though they are an equal part of the team you are all on. Include others as you would want them to include you.

Talk to people at work in a nice, professional way, just as you want to be talked to. Don't start rumors about someone at work just because it is fun to engage in office gossip. Engaging in office gossip can lead to ruined reputations before you even have a chance to realize what is happening. If you don't want someone ruining your work reputation, then don't go around damaging someone else's reputation.

Don't start giving relationship or marriage advice to your friends who are in a relationship or married if you have never been in a relationship or married. Rather, just sit there quietly, listen to them, share their stories, and only start talking once they are done. It is better to just be a listening ear and a caring friend than to advise on things you haven't experienced yourself. No one wants to hear advice on their specific situation when the person giving the advice hasn't even experienced that situation.

PRACTICAL APPLICATION:

In what ways have you placed judgment on someone else at work, at home, or in their personal life?

_____
_____
_____
_____
_____
_____

Have you ever been judged by someone?

_____
_____
_____
_____
_____
_____

In what ways have you learned the hard way not to judge someone?

_____
_____
_____
_____
_____
_____

ENGAGE YOUR MIND:

In what ways did this passage help you understand how important it is to not judge others?

_____
_____
_____
_____
_____

How has God reminded you not to judge someone?

_____

_____

_____

_____

_____

_____

How do you feel after you judge someone? Do you feel better or worse? How did you feel after being judged by someone?

_____

_____

_____

_____

_____

How has this passage softened your heart and helped you realize that if you judge, you too will be judged?

_____

_____

_____

_____

_____

Week 29

FAITH BRINGS JOY

SCRIPTURE READINGS:

Day One: Psalm 16:1 (Refuge in God)

Day Two: Nehemiah 8:10 (Joy of the Lord)

Day Three: Psalm 126:5-6 (Songs of joy)

Day Four: Proverbs 10:28 (Hopes of the Godly)

Day Five: Jeremiah 15:16 (God's words are our joy)

Day Six: Philippians 4:4 (Rejoice in the Lord)

Day Seven: John 16:24 (Your joy may be full)

"Therefore, since we have been made right in God's sight by faith, we have peace with God because of what Jesus Christ our Lord has done for us. ² Because of our faith, Christ has brought us into this place of undeserved privilege where we now stand, and we confidently and joyfully look forward to sharing God's glory." Romans 5:1-2

Take the time to think about what this passage says about you. Look into it and take the time to digest what God is saying to you in it. You were made right in God's eyes through faith, even though you sin every day. God still wants you as His daughter and as His child. He wants to know you on a deep and personal level. You don't have to be tormented by the thoughts of the "what ifs" from your past life since you were made a new creation in Christ Jesus.

You don't have to keep thinking, "What if He doesn't forgive me for the mistakes I've made today?" because He has already forgiven you for the mistakes you have made. You don't have to keep wondering, "What if I make a big mistake today?" because God already knows that you'll sin. He is already there at each one of your mistakes, and He will help you learn from them. He will help you know what not to do and what to do. You don't have to keep thinking that you are doomed because of all the things you have done wrong. Nor do you need to think that God will never accept you.

On the contrary, God still sees you as His perfect and amazing daughter. Because of your faith, God brought you to an undeserved place of privilege in your life.

He loves you more than anyone else could ever love you. He longs to know you and longs to talk to you every day. He longs to hear your prayers and cries of anguish and your shouts of praise. He has prepared a place for you so you can and will join Him and Jesus in eternity in Heaven one day when He calls you home. Instead of dreading things in your life, you can start looking forward to new experiences in your job, home, personal life, and friendships. You can look forward to new experiences every day and every week because they will help you grow into the person that God designed you to be. Every new experience helps shape you into the person you are meant to be.

Instead of looking at new experiences with fear and dread in your heart, you can have the confidence and hope in your heart that were always at the tip of your fingers and only a call away from Jesus. Stop thinking you're no good for your work position, you're not good enough as a mother or wife, and that you could be a better sister or daughter. Instead, start saying these affirmations:

"I am going to excel in this position with God's help."

"I am an awesome mother, and I will continue to be an awesome mother with God's help. I will learn the best ways to parent my kids. My husband and I will work together as a team. We will not play one off of the other."

"I am a good wife for my husband. Lord, please teach me new ways to be an even better wife. Help our marriage soar."

"There is no better sister or daughter than me. God, please help me to be the best sister and daughter I can be through you. Thank you, Lord, that I can have the confidence that I never knew I needed through you. Help me to look forward to sharing in your glory every day and one day when I get to heaven."

PRACTICAL APPLICATION:

How can you share God's glory every day with those around you?

_____
_____
_____
_____
_____
_____
_____
_____
_____

ENGAGE YOUR MIND:

How did God help you realize that just being yourself is exactly who He wants you to be?

_____
_____
_____
_____
_____
_____
_____
_____

How did He help you gain confidence in yourself?

_____
_____
_____
_____
_____
_____
_____

ENGAGE YOUR HEART:

What does it feel like basking in the goodness and glory of God? How does it feel to know who you truly are in Christ?

_____

_____

_____

_____

_____

_____

_____

_____

_____

_____

_____

_____

_____

_____

Week 30

LOVE IS THE GREATEST

SCRIPTURE READINGS:

Day One: 1 Corinthians 16:14 (Do everything in love)

Day Two: John 3:16 (God so loved)

Day Three: 1 John 4:8 (Anyone who doesn't love)

Day Four: Colossians 3:14 (Put on love)

Day Five: John 15:13 (No greater love)

Day Six: 1 John 4:7 (Love one another)

Day Seven: Romans 5:8 (Christ died for us)

"Three things will last forever—faith, hope, and love—and the greatest of these is love." 1 Corinthians 13:13

There are many things that people think will last forever. They might think that the love they have for their families may last forever. They also may think that their love for their spouses may last forever. The scary part is that love can disappear from people's lives at any time. You have to constantly be on guard against losing love for your family or your husband. Love will only last forever if it's eternal love from God. He is the only one who created eternity and everything on earth. God created every person to love others. You are supposed to enjoy fellowship with everyone around you. Love is the most important thing in life. It is the basis for all emotions and actions. When you do something for another person, you do it out of love. It feels good to help someone out of love.

Faith is another thing that people think will last forever. Faith is something that you have to strengthen every day, just as you would strengthen yourself by working out every week. Faith is a muscle that has to be flexed, just as you flex your muscles during a workout. You can sometimes feel the strain that a workout puts on your muscles, and that is the same way that it feels when you "flex" your faith. You will feel the strain of making important decisions in your work life and important decisions for your family. You will feel the weight of the world on your shoulders with finances, family obligations, work, and your personal life. That's when it's the most important time to keep your eyes focused on God. Instead of giving in to the despair that this life sometimes brings, you can rest assured that God is with you through every situation, no matter how hopeless things seem. As long as you keep the faith, you will see God work in your life in marvelous ways.

Hope is another important thing to hold on to in life. Without hope, you won't have anything to strive for. Hope gives you the willpower to hang on even when everything in you is telling you to give up. Hope from God is one of the most important things you can hold on to in your faith walk. Satan has ways of taking your hope away from you, so it is important to know how he can attack you. He can attack you spiritually and make you think that God doesn't care about you. Satan can also make you think that your prayers don't matter and that God doesn't even hear you when you pray. Satan can also attack you mentally and emotionally by making you second-guess your abilities and your God-given talents. Satan can try to make you mentally drained from your everyday tasks, and he can easily get under your skin telling you how bad your life is.

You have to train your mind, body, and spirit to know how to defend yourself against Satan's attacks every day. Instead of giving in to his lies, tell yourself that you are more than capable of doing great things. Ask God to show you your unique abilities and how to use them. Ask Him to fill your heart with His hope in place of any fear that Satan has put in your heart. Show the love of God to everyone in your life and watch how your life changes.

PRACTICAL APPLICATION:

How can you keep faith, hope, and alive in your life?

_____
_____
_____
_____
_____
_____
_____
_____
_____
_____

How has God revealed to you that He is working in your life to keep love alive?

_____
_____
_____
_____
_____
_____
_____
_____

In what ways have you shown God's love to others around you?

_____
_____
_____
_____
_____
_____
_____
_____
_____

ENGAGE YOUR MIND:

In what ways have you been able to resist Satan's attacks in your life and cling to the hope that can only be found in Jesus? Do you truly trust that Jesus delivers you from Satan?

_____

_____

_____

_____

_____

_____

_____

_____

_____

ENGAGE YOUR HEART:

How do you feel when you speak out against Satan and rebuke his attacks?

_____

_____

_____

_____

_____

_____

_____

_____

Week 31

GRACE ABOUNDS

SCRIPTURE READINGS:

Day One: Ephesians 2:8-9 (Saved by grace)

Day Two: Romans 11:6 (Not the basics of works)

Day Three: James 4:6 (Grace to the humble)

Day Four: John 1:16 (Grace upon grace)

Day Five: Romans 3:20-24 (Righteousness of God)

Day Six: 2 Timothy 2:1 (Strengthened by grace)

Day Seven: Titus 2:11 (Grace of God)

"Each time he said, "My grace is all you need. My power works best in weakness." So now I am glad to boast about my weaknesses, so that the power of Christ can work through me." 2 Corinthians 12:9

God's grace is all that you need to support you. Even when you feel like you can't go on in your life, God is still with you. He will carry you when you feel you can't stand on your own two feet. You will feel God at work in your life, even if it's behind the scenes. God's grace is the only reason you have made it this far. Learn to boast about your weaknesses because God's power is made perfect through your weaknesses. Learn to appreciate your weaknesses and embrace them. Once you know that God is helping you overcome all of them in His way and His perfect timing, you gain strength through Him.

Thanks to God, you don't have to see the things that you can't do as weaknesses. Rather you can train your mind to accept that there will be things that you will not be able to do as well as other people can do them. For example, you may not be able to decorate things or organize things in the way other women can. But you can do other things such as possibly run a company, run a charity, or even homeschool your kids. You have unique abilities and talents that other women don't have. Use your talents to the best of your ability. Rejoice in the fact that you are not like every other woman out there. Rejoice that you're different, unique, and talented in your special ways.

Don't be hard on yourself just because you see other women soaring in areas you're struggling in. God wants you to rejoice in your uniqueness. He wants you to be comfortable in your skin. His grace covers all your weaknesses and sins. God wants you to boast that you are saved by Him and through Him. He wants you to boast all the more about your weakness so that His power can be at work within your mind, in your body, and your spirit. Allow God's power to come upon you and allow Him to transform what you see as weaknesses in your life into things you're proud of. Not every weakness deserves your wallowing over it. Some weaknesses are there to keep you from doing things that other people are better suited for. The abilities that make you unique and the tasks you can do well give you something to strive for.

Instead of looking down on yourself for having weaknesses, you can learn to rejoice in your weaknesses because God can and will work through them. You will see God work through them in ways that can only come from Him. He will help you find the best ways to overcome your weaknesses, and He will also help you find new ways to embrace your weaknesses. His power and grace are both made perfect in any weakness that you have. Instead of hating yourself, you can say, "Even though I have this weakness, I know that God will help me through it each time it comes up. I am not weak. Rather I have the power of God resting on me and at work in my life, in any and every situation. I trust you, Lord, that you will help me learn to embrace my uniqueness and that you will help me boast about how your grace has changed my life."

PRACTICAL APPLICATIONS:

How can you learn to embrace any weakness that you have?

_____
_____
_____
_____
_____
_____

What areas of your life do you consider yourself to be weaker than most people?

_____
_____
_____
_____
_____
_____

How can you boast about God's grace and power among your weakness?

_____
_____
_____
_____
_____
_____

ENGAGE YOUR MIND:

How can you change your thinking to boast about God's power even in the middle of fighting your weaknesses?

_____
_____
_____
_____
_____
_____

ENGAGE YOUR HEART:

How do you feel when God tells you to embrace your weaknesses?

_____

_____

_____

_____

_____

_____

_____

_____

_____

Do you truly trust that God's grace abounds in all areas of your life? Do you truly believe that God's power is at work within you?

_____

_____

_____

_____

_____

_____

_____

_____

_____

Week 32

PATIENCE IS A VIRTUE

SCRIPTURE READINGS:

Day One: Romans 12:12 (Be patient in affliction)

Day Two: Galatians 6:9 (Don't give up)

Day Three: Romans 8:5 (Wait with patience)

Day Four: Psalm 37: 7-9 (Wait patiently for God)

Day Five: 1 Corinthians 3:14 (Love is patient)

Day Six: Colossians 3:12 (God's chosen and beloved)

Day Seven: Ecclesiastes 7: 8 (Patient in spirit)

"Always be humble and gentle. Be patient with each other, making allowance for each other's faults because of your love. ³ Make every effort to keep yourselves united in the Spirit, binding yourselves together with peace." Ephesians 2:2-3

Being humble and gentle is something every woman has to work at every day. Some things happen in life, people you encounter, and instances you're faced with where you will no doubt lose your cool in moments of anger and frustration. You will lose your patience at work in front of your coworkers and your bosses. You may say something out of turn and regret it instantly, or you might regret it at a later time when you are forced to think about your words. If you get called into your boss's office, just sit down, listen to the things they're telling you, and only speak up when they are done talking. If they say you're talking out of turn, tell them you're sorry, ask for forgiveness, and say that you take full responsibility for your words. You may have the opportunity to make up for the things you said. Your boss may show mercy to you. If your boss forgives you, make sure you never make the mistake of mouthing off in front of them again. Make every effort to keep the peace and harmony at work.

If you have ever lost your cool in a staff meeting and called out one of your coworkers by saying how dumb, pathetic, or stupid their ideas are, you should go and apologize to them. You should find the time to sit down with them and say how sorry you are for criticizing their ideas. Ask them for forgiveness and if you two can restart on better terms. If they choose to forgive you and choose to try and work with you again, make sure you keep your unwanted opinions of their work to yourself. Try to live in harmony and build up your co-workers by saying that they are doing a great job and that the boss will like their ideas. After all, your coworkers work just as hard as you do to impress the boss. Remember that it is always a better idea to encourage your coworkers than to tear them down. After all, you don't like it when someone criticizes your work, so why criticize someone else's work? Do your best not to find fault with your coworkers and keep unwanted opinions to yourself. Make every effort to be nice to the people at work, and they, in turn, will most likely be nice to you.

You will also lose your patience in front of your friends and family. Whenever you lose patience in front of them, realize where you went wrong. Then come before all of them, asking for forgiveness for your mistakes, actions, and words. Tell them that you didn't mean what you said and that it won't happen again. Do your best not to find fault with your friends or family members because then they will want to be around you more and won't always find fault with you.

You will also lose your patience in front of your kids. Whenever you find yourself losing your patience with them, realize that they are just kids and that they make mistakes just like you do. Tell them that you are sorry for your harsh words and try to be a better parent.

God forgives all of your mistakes every time you come before Him in prayers asking for forgiveness, so how can you not forgive everyone else in your life when they make mistakes? Live with everyone in peace, just as God commands you.

PRACTICAL APPLICATIONS:

What can you do to make every effort to live in peace with people at work, at home, in your family, or around your friends?

_____

_____

_____

_____

_____

_____

_____

_____

How can you have more patience in your life?

_____

_____

_____

_____

_____

_____

_____

_____

ENGAGE YOUR MIND:

In what ways can you change your thinking to be humble and kind to everyone you're around instead of being critical of them?

_____

_____

_____

_____

_____

_____

_____

_____

How have you asked God to change your attitude to want to live in peace?

_____
_____
_____
_____
_____
_____
_____

How do you feel being gentle and humble, forgiving just as God forgives you?

_____
_____
_____
_____
_____

How do you feel when you are kind to unkind people?

_____
_____
_____
_____
_____

Week 33

UNDERSTANDING WHAT REALLY MATTERS

SCRIPTURE READINGS:

Day One: John 14:6 (The way, truth and the life)

Day Two: Proverbs 18:2 (No pleasure in understanding)

Day Three: Proverbs 2:2-5 (Incline your heart to understanding)

Day Four: Proverbs 17:17 (A cool spirit)

Day Five: Colossians 4:6 (Gracious speech)

Day Six: Proverbs 4:7 (Gain wisdom)

Day Seven: Proverbs 20:5 (Man of understanding)

"I pray that your love will overflow more and more, and that you will keep on growing in knowledge and understanding. [10] For I want you to understand what really matters, so that you may live pure and blameless lives until the day of Christ's return." Philippians 1:9-10

Paul was one of the most amazing people in the Bible. A bit of a backstory on him is that he used to be called Saul, and he used to persecute and kill Christians just for following and loving Jesus. He was blinded on the way to a city called Damascus. Then he changed his life and surrendered to Christ to do His work. He became one of the most amazing Christians to ever live. In this Bible passage, he was praying that people would let their love for each other and their love for the Lord overflow into their lives.

He also prayed that the people would continue to grow in knowledge and their understanding of God. He wanted them to understand what it was like to love others in the way that God loved each of them. He also wanted them to understand that a relationship with God was the only relationship that really mattered in each of their lives. He wanted them to understand why loving God was so important so that they could live pure and blameless lives for Christ until the day Jesus Christ returns.

Understanding God takes a lot of work every day of your life, but there are a lot of things that you can do to strengthen and deepen your understanding of God. You can read the Bible every day, read devotionals, and engage with other believers in church every week. You can also worship God at any time, no matter if it's day or night. Just praise Him amid your circumstances, and that will make them easier to get through. You can also read God's word with other believers and share your faith testimony to inspire them. Your story could end up changing someone else's life for the better.

Just as Paul told the people in Philippians that he wanted them to understand what is really important and to be pure and blameless before Christ, you too can gain that knowledge every day of your life. Ask God to reveal to you more knowledge about Him, His ways, His love for you, and for Him to guide you in all of your decisions that you make daily. Ask Him to help you love other people, even when they are hard to get along with. Ask Him to help you learn the best way to stay calm, even in difficult situations, and for you to have more clarity and peace of mind whenever tough decisions have to be made.

You might be asking, "How can I live a pure and blameless life until the day of Christ's return when I sin every day?" God already knows that you will sin every day, but as long as you try your hardest to love people in the way that He loves you and in the way that He loves them, He will smile upon you. As long as you ask for forgiveness from your sins and mean that you are truly sorry and then try not to sin in that same way ever again, He will forgive you. God knows that because of the first sin committed by Adam and Eve, you can't live a blameless life. As long as He sees you trying to share His love, His hope, and His good news of salvation with other people, He smiles on you. Remember, a true relationship with God and leading others to know Him are the only things that matter in your life.

PRACTICAL APPLICATION:

How can you help lead others to Christ through your words and actions?

_____
_____
_____
_____
_____

How have you helped others understand that a relationship with God is what really matters?

_____
_____
_____
_____
_____

ENGAGE YOUR MIND:

What must change in your thinking to live for Him every day?

_____
_____
_____
_____
_____

ENGAGE YOUR HEART:

How do you feel knowing that you are helping lead others to salvation?

_____
_____
_____
_____
_____

How does it feel knowing that you have the power to save someone's life through Christ?

_____
_____
_____
_____
_____
_____
_____
_____
_____
_____
_____

How can you humbly surrender yourself to do God's work?

_____
_____
_____
_____
_____
_____
_____
_____
_____
_____

Week 34

DON'T BE SELFISH

SCRIPTURE READINGS:

Day One: 1 John 3:17 (See people in need)

Day Two: 1 Corinthians 10:24 (Seek the good of your neighbor)

Day Three: Philippians 2:21 (Seek Jesus' interests)

Day Four: Galatians 6:1 (Bear one another's burdens)

Day Five: Hebrews 13:16 (Don't neglect to do good)

Day Six: Luke 6:32-34 (Benefits of doing good)

Day Seven: Galatians 5:26 (Don't be conceited)

"Don't be selfish; don't try to impress others. Be humble, thinking of others as better than yourselves. ⁴ Don't look out only for your own interests, but take an interest in others, too." Philippians 2:3-4

I t takes a lot of discipline not to be selfish. There is something that can make you selfish every day of your life. Some of those things can include getting more assignments than you expected to get at work, having to help your husband with home projects when you have bills that need to be paid, and helping your children with homework after a busy day at work when you just want a little "me" time. You can also want to be selfish when your friends want to go out with you, and you just want some time by yourself after work.

You can also be selfish when you want others to see how good of a person and how good of a Christian you are. You may give generous portions of your money to the church you attend, and you might brag about it to people. But bragging about the gifts you give in the offering isn't a good way to claim to be a Christian. Rather than bragging, you should be proud of the gifts you give in your offering in the stillness of your own heart.

When others tell you that they need help with something, do you immediately offer to help them, or do you say, "I'll help you when I have time."? Giving your time for others helps them know that they are really important to you. It changes your viewpoints and changes your life to view others as more important than yourself. Think back to when you didn't want to help someone else or a time when you didn't help someone right away. Why didn't you want to help them right away? Did Satan make you think that your work was more important than helping them out of the goodness of your heart? Or did Satan make you think that you were more important than the other person?

God also says don't try to impress others. You shouldn't brag about the things that you can do versus what someone else can do. You shouldn't go around with a smug attitude thinking that you are a better person than other people. If you walk around with that type of attitude all the time, you will end up losing a lot of your friends and potentially even have family members walk away from you. No one wants to have a friend who thinks that they are better than who they are. Instead of having that attitude towards people, God wants you to have a humbler attitude and think of others better than yourself. Remember, you are a sinner, just as everyone else is. You are no better than anyone else is on earth. You need help in your life just as others need help in their lives. If you don't help others in their life and during their struggles with faith and life in general, then don't expect them to help you in your moments of struggling with your faith.

God also says to not look out for your own interests only, but to look out for other people's interests too. He wants you to not only care about yourself, but He wants you to care about others in your life. He wants you to act humbly towards other people, not to act proudly or be boastful around them. He also wants you to be interested in the things people tell you and not act as if you already know everything there is to know about life. If you act as if you're better than others and know everything, you won't learn anything new. Ask God to help you become more selfless.

PRACTICAL APPLICATION:

In what ways can you act with a humble attitude towards those around you?

_____
_____
_____
_____
_____
_____
_____
_____
_____

ENGAGE YOUR MIND:

How can you change your mindset from being selfish to being selfless towards others?

_____
_____
_____
_____
_____
_____
_____
_____

How has God helped you change your selfish attitude to a selfless attitude?

_____
_____
_____
_____
_____

ENGAGE YOUR HEART:

How do you feel when you act selfishly versus when you act selflessly?

_____
_____
_____
_____
_____
_____
_____
_____
_____
_____
_____
_____
_____

Week 35

FORGIVE AS GOD FORGIVES YOU

SCRIPTURE READINGS:

Day One: Ephesians 4:32 (Be kind to one another)

Day Two: Mark 11:25 (Forgive others as God forgave you)

Day Three: Mathew 6:15 (If you don't forgive, God won't forgive you)

Day Four: Mathew 18:21-22 (Seventy times seven)

Day Five: Luke 6:37 (Forgive and you'll be forgiven)

Day Six: James 5:16 (Pray with one another)

Day Seven: Ephesians 1:7 (Redemption)

¹² "Since God chose you to be the holy people he loves, you must clothe yourselves with tenderhearted mercy, kindness, humility, gentleness, and patience. ¹³ Make allowance for each other's faults, and forgive anyone who offends you. Remember, the Lord forgave you, so you must forgive others." Colossians 3:12-13

God loves you just as He loves all people. He chose you as His precious daughter. He wants you to be tenderhearted towards people. Even though your work life, coworkers, and the boss will drive you crazy, it means not overreacting. It means being calm in tense situations and only speaking after others are done speaking. When things get out of hand in your home life or you start getting frustrated with your husband, it's important to remember that God wants you to react with a tender heart. He wants you to react with gentleness, mercy, and humility. He wants you to react with kindness and patience. Whenever someone at work or home does something that makes you upset, think about how Jesus would want you to react in that scenario.

He wants you to remember that no one at your work is perfect and that everyone has faults. He wants you to react the way that you would want someone to react whenever you make a mistake at work. He also wants you to allow others to make mistakes and teach them how to better themselves with your leadership at work. He also wants you to quickly forgive others that offend you.

When someone annoys you at home, He wants you to react with love, patience, kindness, and self-control towards them, no matter how angry or fed up you might be. He wants you to make allowances for your family member's faults and shortcomings. He wants you to remember that they aren't perfect and you aren't perfect either. He wants you to quickly extend forgiveness for any of your family members' sins and shortcomings. Remember that you are no better than them and that you make mistakes too. If you can learn to quickly forgive your family members for their mistakes, just as God forgives you every day for your mistakes, you will be more willing to extend grace to them. Then they, in turn, will be more willing to forgive your mistakes and extend grace to you.

Forgiving others is not something that you just learn to do overnight. It is something that you have to work at day in and day out. If you want others to forgive you for your shortcomings, you also have to learn to forgive yourself for messing up and making mistakes. If you can learn to be gentle with yourself for messing up, you will then be able to be gentle towards others when they mess up. Think about it, whenever you sin, you ask God for forgiveness, and He grants it to you, so how can you not forgive yourself? Even more so, how can you not forgive anyone else?

Having humility means thinking less of yourself and more about other people. God thinks the world of you, so how can you not care about your fellow man? God helps you in every situation, so you should want to help others in any way that you can. If any friend needs help, be willing to go the extra mile for them. Remember, God always has gone the extra mile for you, so He smiles on you when you go the extra mile for your friends that are in need.

Clothing yourself with tenderheartedness, mercy, kindness, humility, and patience are all lessons God will help you learn in your faith walk. Ask God to help you have a humble, selfless attitude and for you to want to extend the same grace that He has extended to you to those around you.

PRACTICAL APPLICATION:

What areas of your life do you need to start reacting the way God wants you to react?

_____
_____
_____
_____
_____
_____
_____
_____
_____

How can you forgive just like God does?

_____
_____
_____
_____
_____
_____
_____
_____
_____

In what ways has God helped you learn to forgive others?

_____
_____
_____
_____
_____
_____
_____
_____
_____
_____

ENGAGE YOUR MIND:

What must change in your heart to willingly forgive people?

_____

_____

_____

_____

_____

_____

ENGAGE YOUR HEART:

How does it feel knowing that God helped change your heart to want to forgive others?

_____

_____

_____

_____

_____

How do you feel after you offer forgiveness?

_____

_____

_____

_____

_____

_____

Week 36

PLEASING TO GOD

SCRIPTURE READINGS:

Day One: Galatians 1:10 (Approval of God or man?)

Day Two: Romans 12:2 (The Will of God)

Day Three: Romans 14:8 (Live to honor the Lord)

Day Four: Colossians 3:23 (Work heartedly)

Day Five: 2 Corinthians 5:15 (Live for Him)

Day Six: Mark 16:15 (Proclaim the Gospel)

Day Seven: Acts 17:28 (His offering)

"Finally, dear brothers and sisters we urge you in the name of the Lord Jesus to live in a way that pleases God, as we have taught you. You live this way already, and we encourage you to do so even more. [2] For you remember what we taught you by the authority of the Lord Jesus." 1 Thessalonians 4:1-2

To live in a way that pleases God is important in everyday life. You should want to please God in everything you say and do. You might think that you live for God already and that you don't need to change your life or your habits to live for Him -- that couldn't be further from the truth. There are always things that you can do to live for God every day. Remembering the things you've learned in your faith walk will help you want to learn more about Him every day. There is always something new that you can learn about Him each day.

Living for God means being kind to unkind people, no matter how badly they treat you. It also means being a servant to those around you. This includes your family, friends, coworkers, and anyone who might need your help. Just as Jesus did in His 33 years of life, serving willingly is exactly the kind of mindset that you can have. Living in peace with everyone around you is another thing you can do to live your life according to Christ.

Making peace with the people you find difficult to get along with is exactly what God wants you to do. God also wants you to be quick to forgive people of their mistakes, just as He is quick to forgive you of your mistakes. Forgiving others helps you realize that everyone makes mistakes, including you. It helps you realize how much you need forgiveness too. Be quick to forgive others because then they will be quick to forgive you. That way, you're able to move past the things that were bothering you, and you're then able to make up with each other. It also means calling a truce or a compromise sometimes and being willing to put whatever was bothering you or causing strife between the two of you to rest.

You also have to love others in the same way that God loves you. If you learn how to treat others how you want to be treated, people will treat you nicer. If you love others in the same way that you want to be loved, people will most likely love you back. Even if they don't love you back, just love them anyway.

The most important part about living for God is to share His good news with everyone in your life. You can share His good news by being His example and being a light to everyone in this broken world. You can share your faith testimony with people in your family or friends circle and help others know how God can and will change their lives. Their lives will change forever if they decide to let Him into their hearts and minds.

You can also let them know that living for God every day is not something you just learned overnight. Deciding to live for God every day takes much work and discipline. Tell them that it is a daily choice as to whether they live for God or not. Let them know that their everyday choices can and will affect the rest of their lives. Let them know that they can make the right decisions to follow God every day. Living for God will help them in every area of their life, spiritually, mentally, emotionally, and even physically.

PRACTICAL APPLICATION:

In what ways have you changed your life around to live for God daily?

_____
_____
_____
_____
_____
_____
_____
_____

If you haven't fully surrendered your life to Christ, what do you need to do to change your life around to live for God?

_____
_____
_____
_____
_____
_____
_____
_____

How did God help you change your heart to help you live for Him and be His example?

_____
_____
_____
_____
_____
_____
_____
_____

ENGAGE YOUR MIND:

How can you change your mindset to want to think about God in everything you do?

_____

_____

_____

_____

_____

_____

_____

_____

ENGAGE YOUR HEART:

How does it feel to please God in all you say and do? How has it changed your life?

_____

_____

_____

_____

_____

_____

_____

_____

Week 37

ENCOURAGEMENT DURING PERSECUTION

SCRIPTURE READINGS:

Day One: 2 Timothy 3:12 (Godly life will be persecuted)

Day Two: John 15:18 (Hated Him)

Day Three: 1 Peter 4:12-14 (Fiery trials)

Day Four: Mathew 5:44 (Pray for those who persecute you)

Day Five: 2 Corinthians 12:10 (Content with weaknesses)

Day Six: Luke 6:22 (Blessed when people hate you)

Day Seven: 1 Peter 3:17 (Suffer for good)

What hard times are you going through right now? What hard decisions have you had to make about your personal life, family life, future, or even your marriage? It might feel as though you are in times of tribulation and persecution. How has your faith been strained? Or has your faith been the only thing that you think you can lean on during these hard times? Do you feel as though persecuting you because of your faith in God? Has the persecution made you think about walking away from God or renouncing your faith? This Bible passage talks about Paul being persecuted and thrown in prison. He was eventually sentenced to death for being a devoted Christian leader. Even though you probably and luckily are not facing death or imprisonment for believing in God or talking about Him, it can hurt any time someone makes fun of your faith. Whenever someone mocks you because of your faith, it is hard to forget and hard to overcome.

The good news is that God can and will use the persecution that you face for your faith and for your belief in Him to make you worthy in His kingdom. He knows why people still don't believe in Him, and He also knows when and if they ever will choose to believe in Him. After all, it is God Himself that you're suffering for. He has a great plan amongst the pain that you're suffering while being a witness for Him. He will bring those who are persecuting you for your faith to justice in His timing and in His way. Even though it can be hard to wait for Him to bring those people to justice, remember that He doesn't want you to act rashly against them because He will repay them in His way. Rather, you can tell them that you forgive them for not understanding the things He is trying to teach them.

You can think of it as an honor that you're suffering for the good news of Jesus Christ. You knew from the start of your faith journey that it wouldn't be easy and that this life would be full of trials and strife. God, Himself warned you that you would be mocked and persecuted, just like Jesus was mocked and persecuted. He was even put to death on a cross because people didn't believe in Him.

The other good news that is told to you in this passage is that God will rest for you whenever you are being persecuted for your faith. He will allow you to speak freely about your faith without fear for your safety or your life, no matter who comes against you. He will allow you to have the peace that surpasses all understanding, even amid persecution. You can boldly say, "God, this hurts me, but I know that you are in control. Thank you for allowing me to talk about you, even to those who don't believe in you. I know they are the ones who need you the most." You can also take comfort in the fact that God will provide rest for you when Jesus comes again for the second time.

PRACTICAL APPLICATIONS:

In what ways have you been persecuted for your faith?

_____
_____
_____
_____
_____
_____

Has the Bible lesson helped you realize that there is no greater glory than to stand up and boldly proclaim God's goodness to those who need it most, even if they are persecuting you?

_____
_____
_____
_____
_____
_____

In what ways have you boldly proclaimed your faith?

_____
_____
_____
_____
_____
_____

ENGAGE YOUR MIND:

How can you change your way of thinking about the persecution you're experiencing for your faith?

_____
_____
_____
_____
_____

How has God helped you realize that your faith is worth suffering for?

_____
_____
_____
_____
_____
_____
_____
_____

ENGAGE YOUR HEART:

Does it bring you peace knowing that God can and will give you rest even in the middle of your persecution?

_____
_____
_____
_____
_____
_____
_____
_____
_____

Week 38

INSTRUCTIONS FOR PRAYER

SCRIPTURE READINGS:

Day One: Philippians 4:6-7 (Prayer and supplication)

Day Two: Mark 11:24 (Ask for anything in prayer)

Day Three: John 15:7 (Your desires will be granted)

Day Four: 1 Thessalonians 5:17 (Never stop praying)

Day Five: Romans 8:26 (Wordless groans by the spirit)

Day Six: Mathew 6:6-7 (Pray in private)

Day Seven: James 5:16 (Pray for each other)

"I urge you, first of all, to pray for all people. Ask God to help them; intercede on their behalf, and give thanks for them. ² Pray this way for kings and all who are in authority so that we can live peaceful and quiet lives marked by godliness and dignity. ³ This is good and pleases God our Savior, ⁴ who wants everyone to be saved and to understand the truth." 1 Timothy 2: 1-4

P raying for all people can be a difficult thing to do. Sometimes you just forget to pray because of how busy things can get in your life. Other times, you just don't want to pray for others; praying for others when you don't want to pray for them is the hardest thing to do. Sometimes praying for them is the only way they will be helped out of the situations in their lives. Praying for people in your life can only help them, not hurt them. Asking God to help them can only benefit them in ways you aren't even aware of. Praying for others will change your life for the better too.

Interceding on their behalf is exactly what God wants you to do. Get on your knees and be thankful for those people that God had placed in your life. Pray big prayers for your friends who are going through tough times, and ask God how you can be there for them. Pray for your family that they would see God through your words and actions. Pray for your family and friends to know Jesus on a personal level.

 You may be the only one who even bothers to pray for them, so make your prayers count. Pray for your friends and family that are hurting. Pray for your husband to make it through every day and every week at his job. Pray for your relationship with him to blossom and bloom into the marriage that God wants it to be. Ask specifics in your prayers, and never think that your prayers are ever too small. God hears every one of them.

Pray for your pastors and the church leaders in your home church to make Godly decisions in the church. Pray that they aren't too burned down or exhausted with all of their responsibilities. Pray for a revival for the church and its members. Pray that the pastors would have a renewed sense of purpose in each of their interactions with the congregation. Pray that each of their sermons minister to you and other members of the congregation.

Pray for the nation's leaders. Pray that they would make Godly decisions in their rulings. Praying for the nation's leaders can make a huge difference in how the country is run. It can make the difference that people need. Praying for the country's leaders is a huge step in the revival that needs to occur in this country. When you pray for our country's leaders, you are making it known to God that you care about what happens in this world and the government. You can also give thanks to God for the ability to pray for the nation's leaders. Give thanks to God for the ability to live peaceful and quiet lives marked by godliness and dignity in the United States of America.

It pleases God when you pray for people in places of power and for the people who are directly in your life. He wants everyone to know Him personally and to understand His truth. He wants to reveal His truth to everyone willing to listen. He wants everyone to be saved by His grace and to have an eternal place in heaven with Him. Thank Him that you are making a difference in each prayer that you say. God loves to hear your heartfelt prayers no matter how big or small they may be and no matter who they are for. Take courage in the fact that He hears them all!

PRACTICAL APPLICATION:

In what ways have you prayed and interceded for people in your life?

_____
_____
_____
_____
_____
_____
_____
_____
_____

How can you pray for your family, friends, church leaders, pastors, or nation's leaders?

_____
_____
_____
_____
_____
_____
_____
_____
_____

What do you need prayers for in your life?

_____
_____
_____
_____
_____
_____
_____
_____

ENGAGE YOUR MIND:

In what ways have you changed your thinking about praying for people?

_____

_____

_____

_____

_____

_____

_____

_____

_____

ENGAGE YOUR HEART:

How does it feel praying for people, whether they are in positions of power or not?

_____

_____

_____

_____

_____

_____

_____

_____

_____

Week 39

DO NOT BE ASHAMED

SCRIPTURE READINGS:

Day One: Romans 1:16 (Not ashamed of the Gospel)

Day Two: Mathew 10:32-33 (Acknowledge God)

Day Three: 1 Peter 5:6 (Suffering as Christians)

Day Four: 2 Timothy 2:15 (Handle the word of truth)

Day Five: Mark 8:35 (Lose your life for God)

Day Six: 1 Samuel 2:2 (No one like God)

Day Seven: 1 Thessalonians 4:17 (Caught up together)

"So never be ashamed to tell others about our Lord. And don't be ashamed of me, either, even though I'm in prison for him. With the strength God gives you, be ready to suffer with me for the sake of the Good News." 2 Timothy 1:8

You might be worried about what others may think of you when you start talking about Jesus and the good things He has done in your life. The good news is that you do not have to be worried about what others might think of you for believing in Jesus. You never have to be ashamed to tell others about God. That's what Paul says to you in this Bible passage. Even though he was in prison for declaring God's goodness worldwide, Paul still wanted people, including you, to know there is no shame in telling others about God.

When Satan tries to trick you into thinking that your words and actions for the Gospel and the good news of Jesus don't matter, that is when you need to remember that every action and every single thing you say has the power to either break someone's heart and change their life for the worse or uplift someone and change their life for the better. Satan can also make you afraid to share the good news with others because he can make you think that no one will even listen to you or that you are just one person. That couldn't be further from the truth.

God loves it when you share the good news with the people around you. God loves it when you speak boldly about Him. Use your talents and ask Him for guidance as to whom you should seek out every day. Ask Him what you should say to people and how you should approach them with His words in your heart. Ask Him where you should go to proclaim His good news every day, whether it is only in your town, community, in your church, or out of state, or even out of the country. Even if He leads you to go out of the country on a mission trip to proclaim His good news, don't shy away from that opportunity. Boldly take the opportunity to be a witness for Him no matter where He is telling you to go.

Paul also says, with the strength that God gives you, be ready to suffer with him for the sake of the Gospel. Be ready to suffer for the sake of the good news. Instead of being timid about your love for the Lord, shout it from the rooftops about what He has done for you and the way He has impacted your life. Be ready at any time to suffer many different trials and tribulations for the Gospel and for your faith. If you are prepared to suffer for God, then the pain you will endure will not be as hard to get through. God will give you the strength you didn't know you had in you, mentally, emotionally, and physically. He will give you the courage, strength, and discipline to face each day's challenges head-on with Him at your side. Be ready to suffer for Him at any time, day or night, for the good of His kingdom.

Be a woman that boldly speaks about her love for God at any time and in any place. Be the woman who gladly worships from the rooftops and shouts about God's blessings and the benefits of knowing Him as your Lord and Savior to anyone who will accept it. Even though you will suffer because of Jesus, you will also see the glory of knowing Him on a deeply personal level. The suffering is nothing compared to the eternal glory that you have waiting for you. You have eternity waiting for you.

PRACTICAL APPLICATIONS:

In what ways can you preach the Gospel in your community or across the world?

_____

_____

_____

_____

_____

_____

_____

_____

_____

ENGAGE YOUR MIND:

How has your mindset changed from being nervous to talk about Him to boldly proclaiming His Gospel?

_____

_____

_____

_____

_____

_____

_____

_____

In what ways has God spoken to your heart while spreading His Gospel?

_____

_____

_____

_____

_____

ENGAGE YOUR HEART:

How do you feel when you're preaching the Gospel? How do you feel when people accept God's word versus when they don't accept it?

_____

_____

_____

_____

_____

_____

_____

_____

_____

_____

_____

Week 40

GLORY REVEALED

SCRIPTURE READINGS:

Day One: Hebrews 1:3 (Radiance of glory)

Day Two: Isaiah 49:3 (His glory)

Day Three: John 1:14 (See His glory)

Day Four: John 13:32-33 (God is glorified)

Day Five: John 17:5 (Glorify God)

Day Six: 2 Corinthians 4:5 (Face of Christ)

Day Seven: 2 Peter 1:17 (Honor and glory)

"For the grace of God has been revealed, bringing salvation to all people. [12] And we are instructed to turn from godless living and sinful pleasures. We should live in this evil world with wisdom, righteousness, and devotion to God, [13] while we look forward with hope to that wonderful day when the glory of our great God and Savior, Jesus Christ, will be revealed." Titus 2:11-13

One day, the glory of God will be revealed to us when we get to Heaven. Until that time comes, women are instructed to turn away from godless living and their sin. Instead of giving in to your sinful desires every day, you should live in this evil world with God's wisdom in your heart and mind. You should live devoted to God in every way possible. You should want to live for God alone. You must work at living for God in every area of your life.

It takes discipline to learn to live for God because there is so much sin in the world that can bombard you in every way. For example, whenever you are tempted to do something that you know you shouldn't do, that is Satan trying to mess with your mind and body. He is trying to get you to sin. Whenever you start to feel "good angel versus the bad angel" mindset, that is when the Holy Spirit and Satan are trying to compete for your attention. The Holy Spirit and Satan are pretty much on your left and right shoulder, with Satan on your left and the Holy Spirit on the right. One, The Holy Spirit, is trying to convince you to walk away from the sin you're about to commit, and the other, Satan, is trying to convince you to go through with the sin without thinking about the consequences.

Satan makes you think that sinning is no big deal. He also tells you that sinning isn't really sinning if you have a good time doing it. For example, if you go out with your lady friends and drink too much, Satan can make you think that you won't get hurt or hurt anyone else if you're only a little buzzed and decide to drive. Satan can make you think that buzzed driving is harmless and that it won't affect anyone. However, your inner conscience and the Holy Spirit will automatically speak to your heart, letting you know that you should never drink and drive, because not only is it illegal, it is dangerous, and you could easily end up killing yourself, your friends, and even an innocent person.

Satan can trick you in many other ways too. He can make you think that no one will be hurt by you sinning and that you won't be hurt when you sin. However, you will be hurt by sinning because it affects your knowledge of right and wrong. When you sin once, you may start believing that you can keep getting away with it over and over.

However, when you feel that nudge from the Holy Spirit telling you that you shouldn't be doing something, the Holy Spirit is the one you should be listening to. You were already given the gift of knowledge to know the difference between right and wrong. But God also gives you the free will to choose which path you will choose every day of your life. Make sure your thoughts and actions are in line with God and line with the Holy Spirit.

Whenever you are tempted to make the wrong choices, ask God to help you resist Satan's temptations so that He gives you a way around, or even a way out, of them. You can also ask God for ways to live a blameless and upright life in His eyes. Ask God through prayer to give you ways that you can resist Satan's deception and his foolish charm. Ask God to give you the willpower to resist Satan and for God to help you strengthen your heart, soul, and mind against Satan's attacks.

PRACTICAL APPLICATION:

In what ways can you live a blameless, Godly life?

_____
_____
_____
_____
_____
_____
_____
_____
_____

What do you do to resist Satan's attacks?

_____
_____
_____
_____
_____
_____
_____
_____
_____
_____

How has God helped you know the difference between right and wrong?

_____
_____
_____
_____
_____
_____
_____
_____

ENGAGE YOUR MIND:

In what ways do you mentally prepare for an attack from Satan?

_____
_____
_____
_____
_____
_____
_____
_____
_____
_____

ENGAGE YOUR HEART:

How do you feel when Satan attacks you? How do you feel when God speaks to you?

_____
_____
_____
_____
_____
_____
_____
_____
_____

Week 41

FAITHFUL UNTIL THE END

SCRIPTURE READINGS:

Day One: Revelation 2:10 (Faithful unto death)

Day Two: Ephesians 4:6 (All in all)

Day Three: James 5:16 (Confess sins to one another)

Day Four: Hebrews 5:14 (Powers of discernment)

Day Five: Mathew 28:20 (With you always)

Day Six: Mathew 25:46 (Righteousness)

Day Seven: Revelation 19:7 (Rejoice and give Him glory)

What warnings have you experienced in your life? Have you been warned of potential sicknesses or disasters in your home life? Have you been warned of what could and will happen if you turn away from God in your life? Have you had the opportunity to warn your fellow believers about what could happen if they don't turn back to God? This Bible passage says that you should warn each other because you never know when God will decide to return or when He will call you home. You don't want any of your family or friends to harden their hearts towards God or to be deceived by sin.

Think back to the time when you first believed in God. Remember how much happier you were, how you were more at peace within yourself and with everyone around you? You knew deep in your heart that God was with you in every situation and that you could always turn to Him. But after a while, your faith started to die down.

There are days when Satan can make it seem as if your faith is declining because you don't see progress. Satan can make you want to turn away from God because being a Christian is "just too hard," or "there are too many rules associated with living life as a Christian," or even the lie of "Christians don't get to live their lives, and they don't have any fun."

Satan can make your heart hardened towards God by making it seem as if you can get all the answers to this life by yourself. He can make you think that God will never give you answers to any question that you have. That couldn't be further from the truth. You need God as much as you need air to breathe every moment. You need God as much as you need food and water every day. You also need God to help direct your life every step of the way. Without Him, you will get confused, frustrated, and even angry because things just won't work out the way you thought they would, especially when you're trying to go through life without Him. You will become depressed when you try with all your might, and things just don't play out the way you want them to. You may even start thinking that all your hard work isn't worth it.

However, when you turn your heart, soul, body, and mind back to God, you will find peace that surpasses all human understanding. You will be able to refocus and have clarity on the tasks that used to drive you crazy. You will be able to relax more at your job and in your home life. You'll be able to talk things through in your relationships with your kids and your husband. You will be able to be an inspiration to your friends, family, and even your coworkers with faith in your heart.

With God in your life, you will be able to get through difficult tasks easier. You will be happier instead of angrier. You will be able to enjoy life to the fullest. No matter how hard this life gets, you can be faithful to God until the end. You can trust in Him as firmly as you did when you first believed. You can teach others around you that a relationship with God is the most important relationship they can ever have. You can remind yourself that you will share in the glory of Jesus when you get to Heaven.

PRACTICAL APPLICATION:

In what ways can you share the glory of Christ with everyone around you?

_____
_____
_____
_____
_____
_____
_____
_____
_____

How can you warn others of what can happen if they turn away from God?

_____
_____
_____
_____
_____
_____
_____
_____
_____

ENGAGE YOUR MIND:

How have you noticed your mindset shift when you're focused on God versus when you're not focused on God?

_____
_____
_____
_____
_____

ENGAGE YOUR HEART:

How do you feel when you have wandered from God? How does it feel to come back to Him?

_____

_____

_____

_____

_____

_____

_____

_____

_____

_____

_____

_____

_____

Week 42

APPROACH GOD WITH CONFIDENCE

SCRIPTURE READINGS:

Day One: Jeremiah 29:13 (Seek Him with all your heart)

Day Two: Luke 1:37 (Nothing is impossible)

Day Three: Ephesians 3:12 (Confidence through faith in Him)

Day Four: 2 Timothy 3:16 (Training for righteousness)

Day Five: Ephesians 2: 8 (Saved through faith)

Day Six: John 17:17 (Sanctify them in truth)

Day Seven: 1 John 5:14 (Confidence towards God)

"Let us then approach God's throne of grace with confidence, so that we may receive mercy and find grace to help us in our time of need." Hebrews 4:16

You might be wondering how you can approach God's throne with confidence. The answer is quite simple. You can approach God at any time because He sees you as His beloved child. You don't need to fear being in front of God, no matter how you feel. The other good news is that you can approach Him with anything on your mind, no matter the time of day. He always wants you to boldly approach Him and to tell Him what's on your mind.

You can approach Him with all your feeling, and He will embrace them all. Even if you aren't feeling confident in your life or your faith walk with Him, just be open, honest, and transparent with Him. Even though He already knows all there is to know about you, you can still talk to Him. He wants to have a lasting relationship with you. Let that thought cover you like a warm blanket and bring you peace. You don't have to fear coming before God.

God wants to save you from your sins and Satan each day. He is willing to do all of those things for you too. If you aren't a Christian and want to become one, all you have to do is invite Him into your heart by saying a prayer like this: "Lord, I need you in my life. I accept you as my Lord and Savior. Please forgive my sins, and please help me to not sin anymore. Make me more like You in everything I say and do. Help me to be a reflection of You in everything I do. Amen."

If you are struggling with confidence in your life and your faith walk, you can say a prayer like this: "Lord, I'm struggling with my self-worth and my self-confidence. Please help me to believe in myself the same way that you believe in me and my abilities. Please help me to believe in the unique and special abilities that you have given me. Help me to find my purpose in life and to fulfill it to the best of my abilities. Help me overcome my weaknesses and make me more confident to talk about You to other people. Help me to be more like You in my thoughts, words, and actions. I thank You for being able to come before You at any time with what is on my mind. Help my confidence to grow as I continue to grow in my faith walk with You. I know and believe that I can do all things through You because You give me the strength. Help me to receive Your grace over my life willingly every day. Amen."

You can then use your faith and trust in God to help other believers who may be struggling to approach God. Whenever you see your friends or family members in need, don't hesitate to act. Pray for them and with them as they ask God to help them receive the same grace and mercy that you have found through faith in Jesus. Let them know that Jesus wants to help them in their time of need and that they never have to be afraid of approaching God, no matter what they might have done. Let them know that God wants to hear from them, no matter what they may be going through. Encourage them to come before God and ask Him for grace and mercy in their time of need. Remind them that they can approach God with confidence instead of nervousness. Remind them there is nothing too big or too small for God to handle in their life.

PRACTICAL APPLICATION:

In what ways can you approach God with a newfound confidence in your heart?

_____
_____
_____
_____
_____
_____
_____
_____
_____
_____

How can you help your friends and family learn to approach God confidently?

_____
_____
_____
_____
_____
_____
_____
_____
_____
_____
_____
_____

ENGAGE YOUR MIND:

In what ways have you relied on your confidence instead of God's? How can you learn to trust Him?

_____

_____

_____

_____

_____

_____

_____

_____

_____

_____

ENGAGE YOUR HEART:

Do you believe that true confidence can only come from God?

_____

_____

_____

_____

_____

_____

_____

_____

_____

Week 43

GOD'S PROMISES

SCRIPTURE READINGS:

Day One: Jeremiah 29:11 (He knows the plans)

Day Two: 2 Peter 1:4 (Great promises)

Day Three: 2 Corinthians 1:20 (Promises of God)

Day Four: Psalm 37:4 (Delight in the lord)

Day Five: Joshua 23:14 (Not one promise has failed)

Day Six: Psalm 84:11 (God is a shield)

Day Seven: 2 Peter 3:9 (God is not slow)

"When God made his promise to Abraham, since there was no one greater for him to swear by, he swore by himself, ¹⁴ saying, "I will surely bless you and give you many descendants." ¹⁵ And so after waiting patiently, Abraham received what was promised." Hebrews 6:13.

God made promises to Abraham many times over. He promised Abraham he would have a son named Isaac and bless him with many decedents. He also spared him and his family while flooding the earth. Did you ever think that He wouldn't make those types of promises in your life? You can rest assured that He *has* made those same promises to you. Here are some examples: He promises to never leave you nor forsake you, He promises He is with you through every circumstance, He promises to be your guide, He promises to give you a way out of every temptation, and He promises to bless you and your family. He also promises that even though you'll go through hard times, He is never far away whenever you need help. He promises you that He will always love you, no matter what you may have done.

Since God knew that there was nobody greater than Himself to swear by, He swore by Himself to Abraham. To have God swear by His power and by Himself that things would happen for Abraham must have been an incredible experience. Abraham must have been in complete awe that God was swearing by His power. He had to know that God could and would do everything He promised. You can have that same hope and faith in God in your life, too. After waiting patiently for a while, God granted Sarah the ability to have Isaac even in her old age. In Abraham's old age, God allowed him to be a father again.

Think of the ways that God has spoken to your heart. Has He told you that you would have a son or a daughter, but you weren't sure when you would have a kid? Did you give up all hope of having a child, only to have God grant your request at the most shocking and unexpected time? Were you shocked by the gift of having a child? Even though you may not ever have the physical appearance of God promising you things in the flesh, God still has promised you many things in your life. Think of all the times that He has kept you and your family safe from any harm that you thought would befall you. Because of God's grace and mercy, He spared you from so many hard times.

Just as it says in this Bible passage, you too can be faithful and wait patiently for God to deliver His promise to you, whether you desire to have children or to get married or to have more Godly friends in your life. Whatever you desire, put all of it in front of God, and He will give you the desires of your heart, if and only if it is His will. He will allow those things to happen in your life only if it is His good and perfect will. Remember, those things you pray for may not happen in the way or in the time frame you want them to happen, but if they can happen for Abraham and Sarah, they will happen for you because you have found favor with God. He sees you as His child, and He wants to bless you exponentially in your life. He wants you to come before Him, tell Him what you want in your life, and ask for those things earnestly in prayer, all while firmly believing that you will receive them with all your heart. After you have waited patiently, He will grant your requests.

PRACTICAL APPLICATION:

How can you accept the promises God reveals in your life?

_____
_____
_____
_____
_____
_____
_____
_____
_____

What can you do while waiting for God to reveal His promises?

_____
_____
_____
_____
_____
_____
_____
_____
_____

How can you help people wait patiently for God to work in their lives?

_____
_____
_____
_____
_____
_____
_____
_____
_____

ENGAGE YOUR MIND:

What must you change in your thinking to fully accept God's promises? Do you trust that God will fulfill His promises?

_____

_____

_____

_____

_____

_____

_____

_____

_____

_____

ENGAGE YOUR HEART:

What does it feel like knowing that God has and will continue to reveal His promises in your life?

_____

_____

_____

_____

_____

_____

_____

_____

Week 44

ENTER GOD'S PRESENCE WITH CONFIDENCE

SCRIPTURE READINGS:

Day One: Genesis 3:8 (They heard God walking)

Day Two: Psalm 16:11 (Path of life)

Day Three: James 4:8 (Seek God)

Day Four: Psalm 27:4 (Dwell in the house of the Lord)

Day Five: Psalm 139:7 (Can I hide from God?)

Day Six: Psalm 140:13 (Dwell in your presence)

Day Seven: Psalm 31:19-20 (Take refuge in God)

"Therefore, brothers and sisters, since we have confidence to enter the Most Holy Place by the blood of Jesus, ²⁰ by a new and living way opened for us through the curtain, that is, his body, ²¹ and since we have a great priest over the house of God let us go right into the presence of God with sincere hearts fully trusting him."
Hebrews 10:19-22

D o you struggle with confidence in your life? Do you struggle with confidence in your faith walk? Are you ashamed to come before God? You aren't the only one who struggles with confidence in your faith walk. All believers have struggled with approaching God with confidence at one time or another.

You can have the confidence that you need to enter God's Most Holy Place. God granted you the eternal gift of salvation through His Son, Jesus Christ. Through His blood and sacrifice, you were set free from your sin and freed from hell. What a sacrifice from God Himself! To think Jesus spared you from eternal damnation in hell because He loved you more than anything. Reflect on this -- Jesus allowed Himself to be beaten, whipped, nailed to a cross, humiliated, spit on, and mocked all because He wanted to give you a place in eternity with Him. He endured the beating of all beatings and didn't even resist once because He knew He had to save you and everyone from sin, death, and the power of Satan. There is no greater love than what Jesus has bestowed upon you.

Jesus opened a new and living way for you through the curtain of His Most Holy Place. The curtain is His blood. His blood was shed and sacrificed for you on the cross. He loved you enough to sacrifice Himself for your sins. Because of His sacrifice, you can now have the confidence to come before God and confess your sins. You don't have to be nervous about talking to Him or thinking, "God won't listen to me because of my sins." You can have the confidence to approach Him with whatever might be on your mind.

Ask God to take everything that is burdening you off of your shoulders. Enter His presence with thanksgiving and a sincere heart. Realize what a privilege it is to even be in His presence. To think that you can have an audience with the Great Physician, the Prince of Peace, and the Savior of the world is such an incredible thought. Take it as an honor to be in God's presence. Through sacrificing His body, you were made a new creation in Christ. No greater sacrifice was ever made or a greater sacrifice that will ever be made. Jesus' sacrifice is the ultimate sacrifice. Because of His love and devotion and sacrifice, you can boldly come before Him at any time and have complete faith and trust in Him.

If you have doubted the need to go to church, remember that church is one of the most holy places that you can encounter God and be in His presence. You can go to a church at any time, no matter what you may be going through. You most likely will feel an instant lift in your spirits when you are in front of other believers in worship. There is something amazing about worshipping God. You forget about your problems and the trials of this world for a short time, and you are focused on singing praises to God and learning more about Him. It is important to go to church every week to learn more about Him through fellowship with other believers. You can go into His presence fully obeying and fully trusting Him in everything that He is trying to teach you on a daily and weekly basis.

PRACTICAL APPLICATION:

In what ways have you entered into His presence at church, in your faith walk, or in your daily activities?

_____

_____

_____

_____

_____

_____

_____

_____

In what ways do you need to reenter God's Holy Place?

_____

_____

_____

_____

_____

_____

_____

_____

_____

ENGAGE YOUR MIND:

How do you prepare your mind to enter His presence each day/each week? Do you truly trust that God accepts you as you are?

_____

_____

_____

_____

_____

_____

_____

_____

How can you change your thinking/ perspective about entering God's presence?

_____
_____
_____
_____
_____
_____
_____
_____
_____
_____

ENGAGE YOUR HEART:

How do you feel when you prepare to enter God's Holy Place? Do you feel peace, or are you sometimes nervous about coming before God?

_____
_____
_____
_____
_____
_____
_____
_____
_____
_____

Week 45

BE WARY OF FALSE TEACHINGS

SCRIPTURE READINGS:

Day One: 2 Corinthians 11:13-15 (False apostles)

Day Two: 1 John 1:4 (Don't believe every spirit)

Day Three: 2 Peter 2:1-3 (False teachers)

Day Four: Mathew 7:15 (Beware of false prophets)

Day Five: 2 Timothy 2:3-4 (Endure suffering)

Day Six: Mathew 24:24 (False prophets will arise)

Day Seven: Colossians 2:8 (Human tradition)

"Do not be carried away by all kinds of strange teachings. It is good for our hearts to be strengthened by grace..." Hebrews 13:9.

This Bible passage warns you to be aware of false teachings. It also warns you to stand firm against such teachings. False teachings could come in many forms. There are all kinds of false teachings in this sin-filled world. They could be people claiming to be prophets or the Messiah. False teachings could also mean that people claim that the end is nearer than when it really is. Those teachings could also be people only thinking of themselves or people claiming that God will not come again in His full glory.

It warns you not to be carried away by those teachings or into denial that these false prophets can bring. Those people will try to trick you into believing anything and everything they say. They want to get people to believe what they say for their gain. They want to get as many people to follow them as possible and for people to believe in their cause instead of listening to what it says in God's word. They want to spread false truths about what they believe in. In order to stand firm against those types of people, you have to keep your faith strong.

You can keep your faith strong by asking God to reveal to you which of your life's people are spreading false teachings. Ask God to help you recognize who the false prophets are in your life and what kind of false teachings they are spreading around about God. God will reveal which of these people you need to stay clear of. He will also help you start telling the people influenced by these false teachings and false prophets the real important truth about God. Ask Him for the courage to speak the truth where the other people are speaking evil. Ask God to help those people and their followers see the errors of their ways before it is too late for them. Pray for them that their eyes are opened and that they see that Jesus is the one true God. Only He can save them from their sins, and only He can save them from themselves.

Be brave enough to speak out against these false prophets and their false teachings. Even if you're uncomfortable or nervous about speaking out against them, know that God will protect you from harm physically, emotionally, mentally, and spiritually. You can let everyone around you know that it is not good to be swept in by false teachings or their false promises. You can also let them know that it is good for their hearts, as well as for your heart, to be strengthened by the free grace that God gives to everyone. You can ask the people in your life who they are being influenced by in their faith walk. Then you can tell them that they are being swayed the wrong way by the false teachings of others around them. You have every opportunity to help them back to their ways of living for God.

Be an encouragement to the people in your life who are being swayed away from the faith by the patterns of this world. Offer to pray for them and with them that their faith returns. If you're talking to friends and family members who never believed in God, it's your perfect opportunity to be a witness and to share the true good news of the Gospel with them. God's truth is the only truth anyone should listen to.

PRACTICAL APPLICATION:

Have you ever been swayed away from God by false teachings?

_____
_____
_____
_____
_____
_____
_____
_____

Have you helped people around you understand the difference between true and false teachings?

_____
_____
_____
_____
_____
_____
_____
_____

In what ways can you speak out against false teachings?

_____
_____
_____
_____
_____
_____
_____

ENGAGE YOUR MIND:

What must you change in your thinking to not be influenced by false teachers? How can you cling to God's truth instead?

_____

_____

_____

_____

_____

_____

_____

_____

_____

_____

ENGAGE YOUR HEART:

How do you feel when you hear false teachings? How do you react to them?

_____

_____

_____

_____

_____

_____

_____

_____

Week 46

PERSEVERANCE THROUGH TRIALS

SCRIPTURE READINGS:

Day One: James 1:12 (Persevere through trials)

Day Two: Galatians 6:9 (Don't give up)

Day Three: Romans 5:3-5 (Rejoice in sufferings)

Day Four: 1 Chronicles 16:11 (Seek God's strength)

Day Five: Hebrews 10:36 (Need endurance)

Day Six: Ephesians 6:18 (Be alert with endurance)

Day Seven: Romans 12:12 (Be patient in affliction)

"Blessed is the one who perseveres under trial because, having stood the test, that person will receive the crown of life that the Lord has promised to those who love him." James 1:12

Think back to when you thought you couldn't walk another step, couldn't think about a specific situation, or when you thought there was no way out of a certain trajectory you were on. All of those times, God has helped you through. When you thought you couldn't take another step, that is when God stepped in and carried you the rest of the way until you were strong enough to stand on your feet again. He wants to carry you when you feel like you can't go on because He loves you and only wants what is best for you.

This Bible lesson says blessed is the one who perseveres under trials. They have stood the tests put in front of them; they will receive the crown of life that the Lord has promised to them. You can persevere through all trials that come your way because God is always with you. He has given you the strength, courage, and willpower to get through tough times. Even when it feels as though the obstacles in front of you are too big to overcome, God will give you a way around, over, and even through them. Whenever obstacles arise, remind yourself that you could get through trials before, and you will get through any trials that come your way again in the future.

Remind yourself that you can get through them with God at your side. You have the strength in you to persevere through every trial every time one comes along. Do not cower away in fear whenever trouble comes around, but rather have the strength, hope, faith, courage, and perseverance that can only come through knowing Jesus. You know deep in your mind that God is the only reason that you ever made it through any of the trials that you face in your life. Keep that thought in your mind whenever trials arise and say, "God has gotten me through trials before. I know He will do it for me and with me again."

If you can persevere through the trials that come your way with faith and confidence in your heart, God will reward you by getting you through to the other side. He will continually help you through It all. He will give you wisdom and strength that you didn't realize you had in you. You will receive the crown of life that God has promised you, so long as you keep persevering through trials. Even though life can and will knock you down, you know in your heart that God always has your back. He will guide you through any rough waters. Even on the days when you feel as though you're drowning, God will help you stay afloat. He will help you keep your head above the water. He will never let you down, and He will never let you give up.

Whenever you feel as though you are close to giving up, that is when God comes beside you and whispers in your ear and calms your heart by saying, "My child, I am here with you. I am here for you. I will carry you through this. You are not too weak to withstand this trial. You have my strength already within you. This pain won't last forever. Take my hand and try again. I see you trying your hardest on your own. Now try again with me. We can and will get through this together."

PRACTICAL APPLICATION:

How can you learn to lean on God through any trials?

_____
_____
_____
_____
_____
_____
_____
_____
_____

How has God carried you when you thought you couldn't go on?

_____
_____
_____
_____
_____
_____
_____
_____
_____
_____

ENGAGE YOUR MIND:

In what ways has God revealed His love to you? Have you accepted His unconditional love?

_____
_____
_____
_____
_____
_____

ENGAGE YOUR HEART:

How do you feel when God gets you through another trial, you weren't sure you could get through?

_____
_____
_____
_____
_____
_____
_____
_____
_____
_____
_____

Has He convinced you to walk with Him through trials instead of trying to make it on your own?

_____
_____
_____
_____
_____
_____
_____
_____
_____
_____
_____

Week 47

OBEY GOD'S TEACHINGS

SCRIPTURE READINGS:

Day One: John 7:17 (Do God's will)

Day Two: Psalm 37:4 (Delight in the Lord)

Day Three: Mathew 10:32-33 (Acknowledge God before men)

Day Four: 1 Thessalonians 5:3 (No escape from sin)

Day Five: 1 Thessalonians 4:3 (Abstain from sexual immorality)

Day Six: James 1:22 (Be doers of the word)

Day Seven: 1 Peter 2:15 (Silence fools)

"Do not merely listen to the word, and so deceive yourselves. Do what it says. 23 Anyone who listens to the word but does not do what it says is like someone who looks at his face in a mirror 24 and, after looking at himself, goes away and immediately forgets what he looks like." James 1:22-24

You have probably had one of your bosses say, "Don't just say, 'Okay, I understand.' Listen to what I'm saying and then do as I ask." That's what God wants you to do with His word. He doesn't just want you to skim over it and then say, "Okay, I understand it." He wants you to digest everything that His word says to you. He wants you to understand all the good things and the lessons the Bible offers you.

He doesn't just want you to listen to a Bible study by Joel Osteen or Joyce Meyer and then go about your life as if you didn't learn anything from listening to it. He also doesn't want you to go to church and only half-listen to the pastor's sermons. He wants you to digest everything the pastors are saying and apply those lessons to your life. He wants you to take what you have learned and help other people have the same knowledge.

This Bible passage says anyone who merely listens to the word and doesn't apply it to their lives deceives themselves. So, do yourself a favor and take the time to understand what the word tells you. Learning to listen and understand the words completely offers you many valuable lessons, which you can learn and take with you throughout your life. You can also pass that knowledge down to your kids. When you listen, you'll notice that God offers you stark warnings about how you shouldn't live your life. God doesn't put those stark warnings in the Bible to scare you. Rather, He puts them there so you can have the knowledge of good and bad and the knowledge of right and wrong. If you know the difference between right and wrong, then you can teach the people around you the difference between them.

This Bible passage also says that if you just listen to the word of God and don't do what it says, it's just like looking at yourself in the mirror and immediately walking away, forgetting what you look like. How many times have you tried adjusting your outfit, redoing your hair, or retouching your makeup in the mirror and then gone back a few minutes or hours later just to see how your look is holding up? You want to see if your look is withstanding everything you can throw at it during the day, and if it isn't looking or fitting right, then you do some more adjusting, no matter how long it takes. You want to look good every day for yourself, especially in front of your friends, co-workers, and husband.

The same thing goes for knowing God. If you don't start applying what you have learned about God in your everyday situations, just as you apply your makeup or hairspray, you will forget who He is, what He has done for you, and what He can do in your life. You can also forget that you can always call on Him for help in any situation, and you will start thinking that you can handle everything that life throws at you without His help. If you don't ground yourself in God's word and do what it tells you to do, you will have a harder time getting through things in your life.

PRACTICAL APPLICATION:

How can you apply what you've learned in God's word to your everyday life?

_____
_____
_____
_____
_____
_____
_____
_____
_____

ENGAGE YOUR MIND:

In what ways have you changed your mindset from thinking, "I can do things on my own without God." to "I need God in every situation of my life."?

_____
_____
_____
_____
_____
_____
_____
_____
_____

In what ways has God helped you want to learn more about Him in His word, in church, and your everyday life?

_____
_____
_____
_____

In what ways has God helped you want to keep the lessons you have learned about Him in your heart?

_____
_____
_____
_____
_____
_____
_____

ENGAGE YOUR HEART:

How do you feel when you obey God's teachings? In what ways do you struggle with obeying Him?

_____
_____
_____
_____
_____
_____
_____
_____
_____
_____

Week 48

DON'T SHOW FAVORITISM

SCRIPTURE READINGS:

Day One: James 2:9 (Showing partiality)

Day Two: Romans 2:11 (God shows no favoritism)

Day Three: Genesis 37:4 (Favoritism for Joseph)

Day Four: Galatians 3:28 (God takes no bribes)

Day Five: Ephesians 6:9 (Stop threatening)

Day Six: Leviticus 19:15 (Righteously judge)

Day Seven: Deuteronomy 1:16 (Treat everyone equally)

"My brothers and sisters, believers in our glorious Lord Jesus Christ must not show favoritism." James 2:1

It can be extremely hard not to show favoritism in your life. You can inadvertently show favoritism in your children's lives, which can make one kid thinks you like their brother or sister more than you like them. Or they can also think that you are giving their sibling more leniencies in their life, such as curfews and whom they can hang out with. That can cause resentment between you and your child. It can also cause resentment between your children as siblings.

So, if you don't like it when your children complain about you showing favoritism to their sibling, then you have to be the one who is willing to work at not treating each child differently no matter how you may be feeling towards each one of them on any given day. You have to watch how you treat your kids because they are watching how you respond to them. You have to treat each of your kids fairly, even if all of them are driving you crazy.

You can also show favoritism in your friend group. You can treat your friends unequally and make one friend think that they don't matter to you as much as the other friend does. You can take one out for their birthday while only singing happy birthday to another friend through texts. That can cause resentment between you and your friends very easily. You have to be willing to treat each of your friends the same way, even if one or all of them are driving you crazy. You have to treat each of your friends nicely and never make one think that you like one better than the other. Otherwise, there might be competition between you and your friends.

You can even show favoritism to your other family members over your husband. When you put your family first, instead of putting your husband first, there will be hard feelings and arguments in your marriage because your husband will feel as though he is second compared to your family. You have to take the actionable step to put Him first in all aspects of your life, whether it's finances, family discussions, or figuring out what to make for dinner or where you are going for a date night. Take the time to discuss things with him calmly instead of just running to your mom or dad. If you don't understand why he is a little upset about you always talking to your family instead of talking to him, ask him to explain how he feels in a calm manner. He might explain that he doesn't like that you always talk to your parents about things instead of talking to him about important decisions. You have to be the one who is willing to always come to him first instead of going to your family about important decisions.

It says in this Bible passage not to show favoritism in any area of your life. It is something that requires constant work on your part. You have to work to not show favoritism in your family life, and you have to let your mom and dad go when you are married and out of the house. You have to learn to discuss things with your husband instead of always going to your mom or dad about things. Remember, you willingly got married, so you have to put your husband first before your family or parents. You can learn not to show favoritism in your children's lives by treating them equally and with the same amount of respect.

PRACTICAL APPLICATION:

In what areas of your life have you shown favoritism?

_____
_____
_____
_____
_____
_____
_____
_____

ENGAGE YOUR MIND:

How can you change your mindset to not show favoritism with your parents over your husband?

_____
_____
_____
_____
_____
_____
_____

How can you change your thinking to not show favoritism with your kids?

_____
_____
_____
_____
_____
_____
_____
_____

How do you feel when you show favoritism? Do you need to repent from that?

_____
_____
_____
_____
_____
_____
_____
_____
_____
_____
_____

Do you truly believe God doesn't show favoritism?

_____
_____
_____
_____
_____
_____
_____
_____
_____
_____
_____
_____

Week 49

THE TONGUE IS EVIL

SCRIPTURE READINGS:

Day One: 1 Peter 3:10 (Keep your tongue from evil)

Day Two: James 1:26 (Bridle your tongue)

Day Three: Proverbs 21:23 (Keep your mouth)

Day Four: Ephesians 4:29 (No corrupting talk)

Day Five: Proverbs 15:4 (Gentle tongue)

Day Six: Proverbs 18:21 (Power of the tongue)

Day Seven: James 3:9 (Soft words)

"But a tiny spark can set a great forest on fire. ⁶ And among all the parts of the body, the tongue is a flame of fire. It is a whole world of wickedness, corrupting your entire body. It can set your whole life on fire, for it is set on fire by hell itself." James 3:6

The tongue is the smallest body part, yet it can cause the most damage. One word or one phrase can cause you to lose trust with family members or friends. One phrase can cause you to ruin relationships with those you love. One second you are friends with someone, and the next second, after you say something out of turn, in anger or frustration, the person wants nothing to do with you anymore.

Among all the body parts, the tongue is the evilest one. It is a whole world of wicked thoughts and words that can destroy your life in only a matter of seconds. It can and will corrupt your entire body. The tongue can even set your whole life on fire. That is why you have to be so careful with your words and your actions.

The tongue is a flame of fire, which means it can destroy things faster than the time it takes to build them. It can destroy trust, friendships, and relationships with family members. It can even cause you to lose your job. It can also cause your kids to turn away from you if they feel that you're criticizing them too much. It can destroy your marriage if you aren't careful. You don't want to lose your friends, your parents, your kids, or your marriage just by saying something in the wrong way.

You might be asking, "In what ways can I ruin a relationship in my life?" For example, you can mouth off to your kids when you are angry and instantly say something nasty to your kids that you will regret and have to apologize for later. No matter how much your kids will annoy you, you have to do your best to keep your mouth shut in moments of anger. Keeping your mouth shut is better than saying something that could affect your kids' self-esteem for the rest of their lives. Ask God for peace of mind when trying to talk to your kids. Ask God for clarity when trying to teach your kids important lessons about their lives or curfews. Approach them with love instead of talking down to them.

Another example is when your friends come to you for a listening ear, and you just start giving them advice about how they should approach certain situations with their kids or in the marriage, instead of just listening to them and being the friend they need. If you constantly give them advice, rather than just being there for them when they are going through a hard time, they will not open up to you as much. If you can learn to control your tongue and just be the friend they need, you will keep many more friends. Ask God to help you keep your mouth shut when you feel like advising a friend.

Another example is if you are constantly condescending to your husband or talk down to him, he will get fed up with you. He will probably start talking to you the same way you talk to him unless you start apologizing for the way you're acting. Instead of talking down to each other, you can ask God to help you both work together to improve your life together and to improve your marriage.

Is opening your mouth worth losing important people in your life? Ask God to help you control your words, especially in moments of frustration and anger.

PRACTICAL APPLICATION:

Have you heard and seen the tongue cause destruction in your life?

_____

_____

_____

_____

_____

_____

_____

_____

_____

In what ways can you stop yourself from mouthing off to your friends, family, kids, or your husband?

_____

_____

_____

_____

_____

_____

_____

_____

_____

_____

ENGAGE YOUR MIND:

In what ways has God opened your eyes to the power of the tongue?

_____

_____

_____

_____

_____

_____

How can you control your thoughts better, so you don't speak out of turn?

_____
_____
_____
_____
_____
_____
_____
_____

How has God helped you keep quiet in moments of anger?

_____
_____
_____
_____
_____
_____

ENGAGE YOUR HEART:

How do you feel when you angrily respond to something? How do you feel when you respond calmly?

_____
_____
_____
_____
_____

Week 50

TRUST IN GOD

SCRIPTURE READINGS:

Day One: Isaiah 26:3 (Perfect peace)

Day Two: Psalm 112:7 (Firm heart)

Day Three: Psalm 37:5 (Commit your ways to the Lord)

Day Four: Hebrews 11:6 (Sincerely seek God)

Day Five: Psalm 37:3 (Dwell in the land of the Lord)

Day Six: James 1:6 (Ask in faith)

Day Seven: 2 Corinthians 5:7 (Walk by faith)

21 "Through Christ you have come to trust in God. And you have placed your faith and hope in God because he raised Christ from the dead and gave him great glory." 1 Peter:1:21

Whom do you trust? Do you trust yourself, your husband, your kids, your friends, and your extended family? Do you trust God? Trusting in your friends, family, and even yourself is a great thing, but it can lead to your quick downfall because you can't always save yourself from making mistakes. However, you can teach yourself not to make the same mistakes repeatedly by asking God to help you. God will help you learn not to sin. God will help you to learn not to only trust in yourself. If you trust only in yourself, you'll wear yourself out. You'll also be lonely. Trusting only in yourself can only lead to more downfalls. Your strength will be depleted faster and faster if you only trust in yourself. You will start second-guessing yourself at every turn and questioning whether you are making the right decisions.

Trusting God is the best thing you can do in your life. Since you are a Christian, you can trust God with all your heart. God will save you. You have faith and hope in Him because He raised Jesus Christ from the dead and raised Him to His great glory. Trusting God can save your life, too, because He helps you get through many things that you thought you wouldn't be able to in your life. Having hope in God means having hope that you can and will change your life. Knowing God means that you have hope in your heart, soul, and mind, even in the most challenging and uncertain times. Trusting God means that even though things can and will wear you out, you can cling to the hope and reassurance that God is and always will be with you.

Through having faith in Christ, you can do so much more than you would be able to do if you didn't have faith. You can get through circumstances that you used to not be able to get through. You can walk with the assurance that God has your back, and you can face challenges head-on, even if you are afraid of them. You can get through the challenges with God at your side. Then later, you will look back at those challenges with a bit of nostalgia and a whole lot of happiness because you know you conquered them with God at your side. God gives you the strength you didn't know you needed, and the strength you didn't know was inside you. Through your faith, you ended up discovering that inner strength to help you get through life's unpredictable rollercoasters. With hope, you can face life head-on.

With hope and trust in God, you will be able to do more than you ever thought possible in your life. Hope is what keeps your heart excited for the future instead of dreading it. Remind yourself that when things get difficult, you have the hope of God within you and the hope of eternal salvation in Jesus. When hard times surround you, you will be able to rest in the assurance that you have eternity waiting for you in Heaven. Remember, this world is not your home. You are God's precious daughter, and He gives you the hope that you can find only in Him. God also gives you the eternal gift of salvation freely.

Your faith and hope in God can only benefit you in life. Embrace the hope and trust in God every day, no matter what you are going through, and watch how your life changes.

PRACTICAL APPLICATION:

In what ways have you put your hope and trust in God?

_____
_____
_____
_____
_____
_____
_____
_____
_____
_____

How can you put your hope and trust in God in new ways every day?

_____
_____
_____
_____
_____
_____
_____
_____
_____
_____

ENGAGE YOUR MIND:

How can you keep the hope of God in your mind every day?

_____
_____
_____
_____
_____
_____
_____

ENGAGE YOUR HEART:

How do you feel when you have the hope and trust in God within your heart?

_____
_____
_____
_____
_____
_____
_____
_____
_____
_____
_____
_____
_____
_____
_____
_____
_____

Week 51

LOVE ONE ANOTHER

SCRIPTURE READINGS:

Day One: John 15:12-13 (Greater love has no one than this)

Day Two: Luke 12:33-34 (Where your treasure is)

Day Three: Romans 12:9-10 (Love must be sincere)

Day Four: Galatians 6:2 (Carry each other's burdens)

Day Five: Philippians 2:3-4 (Value others above yourself)

Day Six: 1 Peter 4:10-11 (Use your gifts to serve)

Day Seven: James 2:14-17 (Faith without actions)

"Dear children, let's not merely say that we love each other; let us show the truth by our actions." 1 John 3:18

In what ways have you shown your love to people in your life? Have you shown your love to people through your words, your actions, or even by your reactions to certain situations? You have to ask yourself, are you showing all of those people love? This Bible passage says that you have to work on doing more than just saying you love the people around you. You must show love with your actions.

You have to work on being calm at work. You have to show respect to your bosses and your coworkers. You also have to wait your turn to speak in a company meeting or in a setting where you are one–on–one with your boss. You also have to remind yourself that it is better to be silent than to ever mouth off at your boss or coworkers. Treat each person with the same amount of respect that you expect someone to give you. Don't criticize another employee for sharing their ideas about a company project. Don't speak out of turn when your boss is speaking.

You have to remind yourself not to show any emotions that could cause problems in your work environment. Whenever your boss calls you into their office, your coworker asks you for a favor, or someone wants you to take on some extra work, do not roll your eyes, sigh loudly in frustration, or go to your boss's office with your arms over your chest. Also, do not vent to your coworkers about the tasks that your boss might be having you do. Ask God to help you learn to control your words and actions in your work environment.

When you're at home and see things not being done, do not come at your kids or your husband and let your anger explode. Instead of getting angry and laying into them for not picking up their clothes, folding the laundry, or making dinner, do your best to calmly explain that you need help taking care of the responsibilities of having a house. Those responsibilities for your kids can include washing and folding laundry, loading and unloading the dishwasher, cleaning their rooms, dusting, vacuuming, cleaning the bathrooms, washing the stoves, countertops, and tables after every meal, helping make grocery lists, and then buying the food and supplies that are needed to prepare meals each week. Try your best to approach your kids with love in your voice. Ask them calmly to do each of their assigned chores in a good time frame, so you don't need to keep nagging them about them. Ask God to help you keep a calm spirit whenever you ask your kids with help around the house, so you feel more relaxed, and they won't feel as if you are attacking them all the time.

When you get home after a long day at work and see your husband lying on the couch, do your best not to get so angry with him. Understandably, you want him to be an equal discipliner of your kids. It's also understandable that you want him helping out around the house, whether it means helping take the cars for their oil changes, washing the cars, disciplining your kids when they misbehave, preparing dinner when you are just too tired. Ask God for ways to calmly explain all of those points to your husband with love in your heart. With love in your heart, you will go farther in your marriage than if you were to just come at your husband angrily with hurtful words.

PRACTICAL APPLICATION:

In what ways have you shown love to people you interact with every day?

_____
_____
_____
_____
_____
_____
_____
_____
_____

How can you stop yourself from getting worked up and remind yourself that you need to be more loving?

_____
_____
_____
_____
_____
_____
_____
_____
_____

ENGAGE YOUR MIND:

How can you change your thinking to react to your family, boss, and husband with love?

_____
_____
_____
_____
_____

How do you feel when you react with love to people? In what areas do you need to work on showing love to others?

_____
_____
_____
_____
_____
_____
_____
_____
_____
_____
_____
_____
_____

Week 52

BUILD OTHERS UP IN FAITH

SCRIPTURE READINGS:

Day One: Romans 14:19 (Make peace)

Day Two: Hebrews 10:22-25 (Stir up one another to love)

Day Three: Romans 12:10 (Show honor to others)

Day Four: Hebrews 3:13 (Warn one another)

Day Five: Colossians 3:12 (God's chosen ones)

Day Six: Romans 15:2 (Please your neighbor)

Day Seven: 2 Timothy 1:7 (Spirit of love)

"20But you, dear friends, must build each other up in your most holy faith, pray in the power of the Holy Spirit, 21 and await the mercy of our Lord Jesus Christ, who will bring you eternal life. In this way, you will keep yourselves safe in God's love." Jude 1:20-21

It can be hard to build each other up when you're feeling down. When you aren't feeling like yourself, it's hard to be happy for others. It's tough for you to see your friend's pain when you're wallowing in your circumstances. When you're wallowing in your circumstances, you can become deaf and blind to anyone else's pain.

You have to work every day on building up your friends in faith, the same way you want them to lift you in the faith. Whenever you see a friend struggling in their personal life, ask them if there are ways that you can help them, whether it's just by being a listening ear when they need it the most or by cooking them a nice meal. Other ways you can be a true friend are by taking care of their kids for the day, or even for the weekend, to give your friend a break. You can encourage them by letting them know that God is still with them, even in the midst of their struggles.

It is best to remind them to eagerly await the mercy of Jesus in their lives. Let your friends know that even through their struggles, God is teaching them important lessons. Tell them their struggles will not last forever and that they already have their victory through the Lord Jesus Christ when He calls them to their eternal life in Heaven.

The most important way you can be there for them is by praying for them. Pray on their behalf that the Lord intercedes for them and that He hears and sees all of their needs. You know that the power of the Holy Spirit and the power of prayer is unlike any other powers on this planet. You have seen them both work miracles in life. You know deep in your heart that God is moving in mighty ways through your prayers for your friends. Encourage them to keep their faith strong and to keep themselves safe and secure in God's love.

You can be the beacon of light in your kid's lives, too, whenever they are struggling. Some simple ways that you can do this include offering to help them in their school projects, offering to quiz them before tests to feel better prepared, and cooking them their favorite meal or dessert whenever they are stressed out. You can build them up by encouraging them to follow their dreams throughout their lives. Be eager to help them achieve their goals and dreams by whatever means necessary. Encourage them by telling them that they can and will do anything they set their hearts and minds to.

Pray for your kid's safety and for them to have wisdom in every area of their lives that only God can give. Tell them to never give up on the dreams that God has placed in their hearts and to go after any of their dreams with the courage, strength, and wisdom that only God can give to them. Let them know that some of their best days haven't even happened yet and that their toughest days only make them stronger individuals and stronger Christians. Tell them that they do not have to be afraid to approach you or approach God about anything they might be struggling with. Encourage them and let them know that they always have your support and God's support. Let them know that the best is yet to come and that they can eagerly await the victory that is ahead of them in Heaven, no matter how hard things may seem in the present moment.

PRACTICAL APPLICATION:

In what ways have you built up the people in your life?

_____
_____
_____
_____
_____
_____
_____
_____
_____
_____

In what ways can you build others up in the love of God?

_____
_____
_____
_____
_____
_____
_____
_____
_____
_____
_____

How can you open your heart to love others amidst your suffering?

_____
_____
_____
_____
_____
_____
_____
_____
_____

ENGAGE YOUR MIND:

How does God remind you to never be blind to other people's pain even if you're suffering?

_____

_____

_____

_____

_____

_____

_____

_____

_____

_____

ENGAGE YOUR HEART:

How do you feel being there for others even if you're going through a tough time?

_____

_____

_____

_____

_____

_____

_____

_____

_____

_____

Conclusion

After reading this women's study Bible, we hope that you feel empowered to conquer any challenges that come your way through God's eternal love and guides. It has been our goal for you to feel enriched and enlightened after studying each lesson. At this point, I hope you can look back on each lesson and of the questions that you answered with a new sense of purpose inspired by strengthening your connection to God. By applying each lesson to your daily life, there is nothing you can't get through with God at your side, as you've seen through the course of this past year.

Remember, the more you learn about Him each week, the more you will want to know Him. You can be filled with hope, gratitude, and joy every day, as long as you keep your eyes on Him and keep the faith. Keeping up with your study Bible lessons will continue to give you a deeper understanding of God and His plan for your life. We hope that this study Bible has enriched your mind and your soul, becoming a blessing to your life of faith. You can continue to read it whenever you need to recommit to your path as a devoted Christian.

May you always have oneness with God.